5-Minute

Devotional

for Teen Girls

A 52-Week Faith Journey to Build
Confidence, Find Joy in Christ, and
Discover Your God-Given Purpose

Robin Kite

For my daughter, Texa

Your life continues to show me what it means to love with my whole heart, to find joy in the smallest moments, and to trust God even when the path is hard. Even though you are no longer here with me, your light is still shining. It shines through every word I write, every teenage girl who turns these pages, and every heart touched by this devotional.

Your story lives on in hope. It lives on in faith. And it keeps pointing us back to Jesus, the One who holds us both.

I carry you with me always.

Unless otherwise indicated, all biblical citations were taken from the New Living Translation of the Holy Bible.

Table of Contents

Introduction

Welcome! I'm so glad you're here. If you're reading this, it means you're ready to take a step toward discovering who you truly are in Christ and learning to live as the daughter of a King.

Let's be honest: being a teenager isn't easy. There's pressure to fit in, to look perfect, and to have it all together. However, God's Word tells a different story about you. You're not defined by grades, likes, or other people's opinions. You're defined by the One who created you, loves you deeply, and calls you His own.

This devotional was written with you in mind: your hopes, your questions, and your everyday moments. Each week will meet you right where you are, whether you're walking through friendship struggles, facing self-doubt, or simply needing a reminder of who you are in Christ.

Here's what you'll find inside:

Real talk: Honest reflections about the things you face every day.

God's truth: Scripture to help you hear His voice above the noise.

Encouragement: A reminder that you are loved, chosen, and never alone.

As you read, remember this: you don't have to earn God's love or try to be enough. You already are. You are seen, valued, and deeply loved by the One who calls you His daughter.

So take a deep breath, quiet your heart, and open yourself to what God wants to show you. My prayer is that through these pages, you'll grow in confidence, faith, and peace as you discover what it means to live every day as a true **Daughter of the King.**

With love,

Robin.

How to Use This Devotional

There's no perfect way to do a devotional, but these simple steps can help you make the most of your time with God.

1. Set a Consistent Time

Even five quiet minutes a day can make a difference. Choose a time that works best for you: morning, lunch, or before bed. The goal is consistency, not perfection.

2. Find a Quiet Space

Pick a place where you can focus: your room, a favorite chair, or a quiet corner. Bring your Bible, this book, and a journal if you have one.

3. Start with Prayer

Before reading, pause and pray:

God, help me hear You today. Speak to my heart and show me what You want me to know.

4. Read Slowly and Reflect

Don't rush. Read each verse and reflection with your heart open. When something stands out, underline it or jot it down. God often speaks in small, quiet moments.

5. Write and Apply

Use the reflection space to write your thoughts, hopes, and prayers. Ask yourself, "How can I live this out today?" Small steps lead to lasting change.

6. Give Yourself Grace

If you miss a day, start again tomorrow. God's mercies are new every morning, and He cares more about your heart than your perfect record.

7. Celebrate Growth

Look back often and notice how God is working in your life. Write down answered prayers, new insights, or ways you're changing.

This devotional is about slowing down, listening, and letting God remind you of who you are in Him. Take it one day at a time, and trust that He's shaping you into the strong, kind, and hopeful young woman He created you to be.

Note to Parents or Youth Leaders

This devotional was created to help teenage girls discover who they are in Christ and to grow in faith, confidence, and emotional strength through God's Word. Parents, mentors, and youth leaders are invited to come alongside them on this journey; to read together, discuss the reflection prompts, and create space for honest conversations about faith and identity.

Your presence matters more than you know. When you listen, share your experiences, and remind them of God's love, you help their faith take root in real life. Through your encouragement and example, they begin to see that following Jesus isn't just something we talk about; it's a way of living every day with purpose, hope, and confidence in who He says we are.

Week 1

I Am Loved

"The LORD appeared to us in the past, saying: 'I have loved you with an everlasting love; I have drawn you with unfailing kindness. "
Jeremiah 31:3

Have you ever felt like you're just not enough? Maybe you scroll through social media and wonder why everyone else seems so confident, so pretty, so put together. Or perhaps a friend suddenly stops talking to you, and you can't help but replay every moment, wondering what you did wrong.

It's easy to start believing the lie that love has to be earned, that you have to prove your worth to be accepted. But here's the truth: **God's love for you has nothing to do with how perfect you are**. It's not based on your looks, your grades, your followers, or even the mistakes you've made. His love is steady, constant, and unshakable.

Even on the days when you feel invisible or unwanted, God is still there, whispering to your heart, *"I love you. I choose you."* You don't have to chase His approval because it's already yours.

Take a deep breath and let this truth sink in: **"God loves me with an everlasting love, and His kindness will never fail me."**

Let those words quiet the noise of comparison and self-doubt. You are more than enough, not because of what you do, but because of *Who loves you.*

Reflection

1. When was the last time you felt like you didn't measure up? What caused that feeling?

2. How do you usually respond when you feel unloved or left out?

3. What would it look like to honestly believe that God's love never changes, no matter what?

4. Can you think of a moment when you felt God's love in your life, even in a small way?

5. What's one thing you can do this week to remind yourself that you are deeply loved by God?

Even when people let you down, **God's love never will**. His kindness follows you into every class, every conversation, and every quiet moment when you start to doubt your worth.

No matter what happens today, hold on to this truth: **You are loved. Completely. Endlessly. Unconditionally.**

Faith in Action Challenge

Write a short note or text to someone who might need encouragement this week. Remind them that they are loved and seen by God. You will be surprised by how sharing love helps you feel it even more deeply.

Week 2

I Am Worthy

"Are not five sparrows sold for two pennies? Yet not one of them is forgotten by God. Indeed, the very hairs of your head are all numbered. Do not be afraid; you are worth more than many sparrows."
Luke 12:6–7

Have you ever felt invisible, like no one really sees you, knows you, or even cares about what you are going through? Maybe you have felt lost in the crowd at school, overlooked by friends, or like your struggles do not matter to anyone.

Here is the incredible truth: **God sees you. He knows you. And He values you more than you can imagine.**

Jesus used the example of sparrows, tiny birds most people barely notice, to show how much God cares about even the smallest details of His creation. If He does not forget a single sparrow, imagine how much more He cares about you.

God knows everything about you, even the number of hairs on your head. He sees your tears, your fears, and your dreams. You are never invisible to Him.

The best part? **Your worth is not based on your grades, your looks, or how many followers you have.** It is based on the powerful truth that you belong to Him. You are deeply loved, fully known, and infinitely valuable.

Take a quiet moment to let that truth settle in: **"God sees me, knows me, and values me. I do not have to be afraid."**

Write down one thing you have been afraid to bring to Him, maybe a worry, a mistake, or a hidden dream. Give it to God and remind yourself that you are completely seen and completely loved.

Reflection

1. What is one area of your life where you feel unseen or under-valued?

____

____

____

2. How does it change your perspective to know that God sees you, knows you, and values you deeply?

____

____

____

3. When have you felt truly seen or appreciated by someone? How did that moment make you feel?

____

____

____

4. What is one lie you have believed about your worth, and how can you replace it with the truth of God's love?

____

____

____

5. How can you remind yourself of God's care when you start to feel invisible or unimportant?

____

____

____

You are never invisible to God. He sees every detail of your life, knows your heart, and values you more than you can imagine.

Your worth is not something you have to earn or prove. It has already been decided by the One who made you.

Even when you feel overlooked or forgotten, hold on to this truth: **You are seen. You are known. You are worthy.**

Faith in Action Challenge

Write *"I am seen. I am known. I am worthy"* on a sticky note or make it the lock screen of your phone. Each time you see it this week, thank God for how deeply He values you just as you are.

Week 3

I Am Strong

"I can do all things through Christ who strengthens me."
Philippians 4:13

Have you ever faced something that felt completely overwhelming? Maybe it is the pressure of upcoming exams that makes your stomach turn, friendship drama that keeps you up at night, or a personal struggle that makes you feel like you are barely holding it together. You look at everything happening and think, *"I just do not have what it takes."*

Here is the truth that can completely shift your perspective: **Your strength does not come from how capable, confident, or put-together you are. Real strength comes from Christ living in you.**

When Paul wrote this verse, he was not sitting somewhere comfortable, bragging about his abilities. He was actually in prison, facing some of the hardest days of his life. Yet even there, he discovered something powerful. **Christ's strength in him was more than enough** to handle anything he faced.

Think about what that means for you. The same power that raised Jesus from the dead lives in you. That strength is not just for the 'big' life-or-death moments, it is for your everyday battles too, the anxiety before a test, the courage to walk away from gossip, the confidence to speak up for what is right, and the endurance to keep going when you feel like quitting. **Christ's strength meets you in all of it.**

Take a moment today to name one challenge that feels too big for you right now. Write it down, and beside it, write **Philippians 4:13.** Before you face that thing, whether it is today, tomorrow, or next week, pause and pray. Ask Jesus to be your strength. Picture Him standing beside you, His power flowing through you. Then take the first step, not in your own strength, but in His.

Say this out loud: **"I can do all things through Christ who strengthens me. I am not facing this alone. His power is in me, and that makes me strong."**

Let this truth replace your *"I can't"* with His *"You can through Me."*

Reflection

1. What challenge are you facing right now that makes you feel weak or not enough?

____

____

2. Can you think of a time when God gave you strength to get through something hard?

____

____

3. What is the difference between trying to be strong on your own and leaning on Christ's strength?

____

____

4. When you feel overwhelmed, how do you usually cope? Do those ways draw you closer to God or away from Him?

____

____

5. What is one practical way you can invite Christ's strength into your life this week?

____

____

You do not have to be strong on your own, and that is good news. Jesus does not expect you to have it all together. He asks you to lean on Him. Every challenge you face is a chance to experience His strength working through you.

When you start to feel weak, remind yourself that **you are strong, not because of who you are, but because of Who lives in you.**

Faith in Action Challenge

Write *"I can do all things through Christ who strengthens me"* on a mirror, notebook, or sticky note. Each time you see it this week, say it out loud as a reminder that His strength is always with you, even in the small moments.

Week 4

I Am Brave

"Be strong and courageous. Do not be afraid or terrified because of them, for the LORD your God goes with you; He will never leave you nor forsake you."
Deuteronomy 31:6

What is something you have been avoiding because you are scared? Maybe it is speaking up when you see something wrong, trying out for a team, sharing your faith with friends, ending a toxic friendship, or simply being yourself instead of who everyone expects you to be.

Fear has a way of making us play it safe, stay quiet, blend in, and shrink back from the opportunities God has placed before us. But here is the truth about courage: **bravery is not about being fearless; it is about trusting God more than you trust your fear.**

When God told the Israelites to *"be strong and courageous,"* they were about to face powerful enemies and overwhelming challenges. He was not saying they would not feel fear; He was reminding them that **He would be with them.** Real courage does not mean never feeling afraid. It means you move forward anyway, believing God is beside you every step of the way.

Think about what God promises here: **He goes with you.** Not just ahead of you or behind you, but right there in the middle of your situation, every step, every moment. And He will never leave you; not when you mess up, not when things get hard, not when you feel alone. **His presence is your courage.**

Take a moment today to name the fear that has been holding you back. Be honest with God about it. Write it down or say it out loud. Then, before you take any brave action, remind yourself of His promise: **"The Lord my God goes with me. He will never leave me."**

You do not have to feel brave to *be* brave. Take one small courageous step this week; maybe speaking up, starting something new, or standing firm in your faith. Before you act, whisper this truth over yourself: **"I am brave, not because I have no fear, but because God is with me. He will never leave me. His presence gives me courage."**

Let His promise be bigger than your fear.

Reflection

1. What fear has been holding you back from something you know God wants you to do?

----

2. Can you remember a time when you did something brave even though you were scared? How did God show up for you in that moment?

----

3. What is the difference between being brave on your own and being courageous with God by your side?

----

4. How does knowing that God will never leave or forsake you change the way you face scary situations?

----

5. What is one small, brave step you can take this week that honors God and pushes you outside your comfort zone?

Bravery is not the absence of fear. It is about choosing to trust God in the middle of it. You do not have to have everything figured out or feel completely confident before you act. **God's presence goes with you into every challenge, every conversation, and every new beginning.**

Even when fear tries to hold you back, remember: **You are brave, not because you are fearless, but because God is with you.** And that changes everything.

Faith in Action Challenge

Do one small thing this week that scares you, but do it *with* God. Before you act, pause and pray, "God, go with me." Then step forward knowing He is right there beside you.

Week 5

I Am Kind

"Be kind and compassionate to one another, forgiving each other, just as in Christ God forgave you."
Ephesians 4:32

Have you ever snapped at someone and instantly wished you could take it back? Maybe your little sibling was getting on your nerves, a friend said something hurtful, or someone at school pushed your last button. In those moments, kindness can feel impossible. But here is the thing: **kindness is not just an admirable personality trait. It is a strength that can change hearts, including your own.**

The truth is, genuine kindness flows from knowing how deeply you have already been forgiven. God did not wait for you to be perfect before He loved you. He showed compassion when you did not deserve it, forgave you when you messed up, and continues to show you grace every single day. When you understand how kind God has been to you, it becomes easier to pass that kindness on, even to people who may not deserve it.

Kindness and forgiveness go hand in hand. When you hold grudges or snap back in anger, it is like carrying heavy weights that drag you down. But when you choose compassion and forgive, just as Christ forgave you, you set yourself free. Your heart becomes lighter, and God's love flows through you more easily.

Today, let kindness be your strength. Think of someone who has been difficult lately, someone who has hurt you, annoyed you, or let you down. Write their name down, then pray, **"God, help me show them the same kindness and forgiveness You have shown me."**

Commit to one small act of kindness today. It does not have to be big. Offer a genuine smile, send a kind message, help someone out, or choose not to gossip when everyone else does.

Say this out loud: **"I am kind because God has been kind to me. I forgive because I have been forgiven."**

Watch how this simple choice changes your mood, your relationships, and your heart.

Reflection

1. Can you remember a time when someone's kindness made your day better? What did they do, and how did it make you feel?

2. Who in your life is hardest to be kind to right now? Why is it such a challenge?

3. How does holding onto anger or refusing to forgive end up hurting you more than the other person?

4. When you think about how God has forgiven you, how does that inspire you to treat others differently?

5. What is one way you can intentionally show more compassion this week at home, at school, or with your friends?

Kindness is not weakness. It is a **strength rooted in the love of Christ.** Every time you choose compassion over cruelty, forgiveness over bitterness, and grace over judgment, you show the world a glimpse of God's heart.

Your kindness has power. It can heal, encourage, and remind people that they matter. Let His kindness flow through you today and watch how it changes everything.

You are kind because He has been kind to you.

Faith in Action Challenge

Do one unexpected act of kindness this week. Hold the door for someone, offer a compliment, help a classmate, or send an encouraging text. Let God's love shine through your small, simple actions.

Week 6

I Am Grateful

"Give thanks in all circumstances, for this is God's will for you in Christ Jesus."
1Thessalonians 5:18

Have you ever had one of those days when everything feels wrong? Maybe you failed a test you studied hard for, got into an argument with your best friend, or your parents don't seem to understand you. When life feels messy or unfair, being grateful is probably the last thing on your mind.

Here is the secret that can change everything: **gratitude is not just for the good days; it is how you discover God's goodness in the hard ones, too.**

Gratitude is a choice that transforms how you see your life. Notice that the verse does not say *"give thanks for all circumstances,"* but *"give thanks in all circumstances."* That means even when things do not go your way, you can still find something to thank God for—a caring text from a friend, a peaceful walk, a warm bed, or a second chance. When you train your heart to notice these small gifts, even ordinary days begin to feel extraordinary.

Think about it. Your teen years are full of ups and downs, drama, pressure, joy, disappointment, excitement, and everything in between. But every moment, good or bad, is still a gift. **Choosing gratitude does not mean ignoring your problems; it means trusting that God is still good, even when life is not easy.** Gratitude shifts your focus from what is missing to what is right in front of you.

Today, practice seeing your world through grateful eyes. Grab your phone or journal and set a timer for two minutes. Write down everything you are thankful for, big or small. Do not overthink it. Just let it flow—your favourite hoodie, your best friend's laugh, hot showers, forgiveness, music, coffee, and second chances.

When the timer stops, look at your list and pray: **"God, thank You for these gifts. Help me remember Your goodness even when life gets hard."**

Then set a reminder to do it again tomorrow. Watch how this simple habit begins to change your heart.

Reflection

1. What are three specific things you are grateful for today, especially small details you might usually overlook?

----

2. Think about something hard you are going through right now. Can you see even one small blessing hiding in it?

----

3. How does focusing on what you have instead of what you lack change your attitude?

----

4. Who is someone you could thank this week for their kindness or support?

----

5. What might happen if you made gratitude a daily habit instead of something you only practice when life feels good?

Gratitude is not pretending everything is perfect. It is remembering that **God is still present and good, even when life is not.** When you choose thankfulness, you are declaring that His blessings are greater than your struggles.

No matter what today brings, pause and notice the good. **Let gratitude be your strength, turning ordinary moments into reminders of God's extraordinary love for you.**

Faith in Action Challenge

Start a "Gratitude Note" on your phone or in your journal. Each day this week, add three things you are thankful for. At the end of the week, look back and see how God has been at work, even in the little things.

Week 7

I Am Blessed

"Taste and see that the Lord is good; blessed is the one who takes refuge in Him."
Psalm 34:8

Have you ever felt like everyone else's life is better than yours? Maybe you scroll through social media and see friends travelling, hanging out in perfect friend groups, or living out the goals you have been dreaming about. It is so easy to focus on what you do not have and miss the blessings right in front of you entirely.

Here is the truth that can change your perspective: **your life is already overflowing with blessings, even when it does not feel like it.**

The psalmist says, *"Taste and see that the Lord is good."* That is not just a casual suggestion; it is an invitation. It means you have to intentionally look for God's goodness, notice it, and savour it, just like you would your favourite meal. When you take refuge in God, choosing to run to Him rather than away from Him in hard times, you discover something powerful: **you are blessed not because life is perfect, but because God is good.**

Think about it. Blessings do not always show up in obvious ways. Sometimes they look like a friend who texts you right when you need encouragement, a sunrise that makes you stop and smile, a hard lesson that helps you grow, or the quiet strength that gets you through a tough day. When you lean on God as your safe place, you begin to see blessings everywhere, even in the middle of struggle.

Today, open your eyes to the blessings around you. Take a short *"blessing walk."* Walk through your room, your house, or even your school, and intentionally look for signs of God's goodness. Maybe it is your favourite cozy spot, a photo of someone who loves you, your health, your talents, or just the fact that you are breathing. As you notice each one, pause and say out loud, **"Thank You, God,**

for this."

Then write down the biggest blessing you discovered. Underneath it, write this reminder: **"I am blessed because God is good, and He is my refuge."**

Keep that note somewhere you will see it often, especially on the hard days. Let it remind you that God's blessings are always closer than you think.

Reflection

1. What does it mean to take refuge in God in your daily life? How can you turn to Him when things feel overwhelming?

2. Can you think of a recent blessing, big or small, that helped you through a tough moment?

3. Why is it so easy to notice what is missing instead of what is present?

4. How might your outlook change if you treated every day as a gift instead of something to get through?

5. Who in your life feels like a blessing from God, and when was the last time you told them?

You are blessed not because your life is perfect, but because **God's goodness never changes.** Even when things are messy, His blessings surround you like sunlight breaking through the clouds. When you train your heart to *"taste and see"* His goodness, everything begins to shift.

Ordinary moments start to feel sacred. Hard days become proof that God's strength is real, and taking refuge in Him becomes your most incredible blessing of all.

You are blessed because He is good and with you.

Faith in Action Challenge

Take a few minutes today to send a thank-you message to someone who has been a blessing in your life. Let them know how much their friendship, encouragement, or kindness means to you. It might bless them, too.

Week 8

I Am Joyful

"Do not grieve, for the joy of the Lord is your strength."
Nehemiah 8:10

Have you ever felt like your joy has been stolen? Maybe you are walking through a season filled with friendship drama, family stress, or disappointments that keep piling up. The world feels heavy, and even smiling feels like work. You might even feel guilty for not being as *happy* as everyone else seems to be.

Here is the truth that can completely shift your outlook: **the joy of the Lord is not based on how perfect life is. It is the strength that carries you through when life isn't.**

This is not about faking happiness or pretending everything is fine. **True joy runs deeper.** It is a well of peace and hope that comes from knowing God is with you, even in your most challenging moments. When life tries to dim your light, His joy becomes the strength that keeps it shining.

Think about it. Happiness depends on what happens around you, but joy comes from *Who* is within you. You do not have to create joy on your own; it is a gift God gives you. His joy does not erase your problems, but it fills your heart with strength to face them. It lifts your spirit when you feel drained, renews your hope when things look dark, and can even bring a genuine smile back to your face.

Today, let God's joy fill your heart and overflow into your day. Grab your journal or open your notes app and create a *"Joy List."* Write down five things that genuinely make you happy, things that remind you of God's goodness. It may be your favorite worship song, laughing with your best friend, your pet's goofy energy, or that first sip of coffee in the morning. These are not distractions from your problems; they are reminders that God's joy remains, even when life feels uncertain.

Then say this out loud: **"The joy of the Lord is my strength. His joy lifts me up and carries me through."**

Let that truth settle deep in your heart and remind you that joy is yours, not someday, but today.

Reflection

1. When was the last time you felt genuinely joyful? What made that moment special?

----

2. What is the difference between happiness, which depends on circumstances, and joy, which comes from God?

----

3. On your hardest days, what tends to steal your joy: comparison, disappointment, worry, or something else? How can you guard your heart against it?

----

4. Who in your life radiates joy even in tough times? What do you think helps them stay that way?

----

5. How could you share God's joy with someone who is struggling this week?

The joy of the Lord is not just a nice thought. **It is your strength.** When you are exhausted, discouraged, or overwhelmed, His joy becomes the fuel that helps you keep going. It is the quiet hope that whispers, *"This is not the end of your story."* It is the resilience that enables you to rise again when life knocks you down.

Do not wait for everything to be perfect to experience joy. **Choose joy today, not because life is easy, but because God is with you.**

Faith in Action Challenge

Spread joy this week. Send an encouraging text, share your favorite worship song, or surprise someone with a small act of kindness. Let God's joy flow through you and brighten someone else's day.

Week 9

I Am Calm

"Peace I leave with you; my peace I give you. I do not give to you as the world gives. Do not let your hearts be troubled and do not be afraid."
John 14:27

Do you ever feel like your mind will not stop racing? Maybe you lie awake at night replaying a conversation, worrying about tomorrow's test, stressing about what people think, or feeling anxious about things you cannot control. The world feels chaotic and overwhelming, and peace seems impossible. Your heart is troubled, and you are tired of pretending it is not.

Here is the truth Jesus wants you to know: **He offers you a peace that the world cannot touch.**

The world's version of peace depends on everything going right—good grades, great friendships, perfect plans. But the peace Jesus gives is different. His peace stays steady even when life feels messy or uncertain. It is not about your *situation* being calm; it is about your *heart* being quiet, no matter what is happening around you.

Think about it; Jesus spoke these words to His disciples right before one of the hardest nights of their lives. He knew fear and chaos were coming, yet He still promised them peace. That was not denial or pretending. It was a supernatural calm rooted in trust.

When worry starts to creep in about school, friends, family, or the future, you can pause, take a deep breath, and let His peace meet you right where you are.

Today, take time to receive the gift of Jesus' peace. Find a quiet spot, set a timer for five minutes, and close your eyes. Take slow, deep breaths and focus on this truth: **Jesus has already given you His peace.** With each breath in, imagine drawing in His calm. With each breath out, picture releasing your worries to Him.

If your mind starts to wander, gently bring it back to His promise:

"My peace I give you."

Then say this out loud: **"Jesus' peace is mine. I do not have to be troubled or afraid. His calm settles my heart."**

Reflection

1. What situations or thoughts make you feel the most anxious or overwhelmed?

----

2. When your heart starts to race with worry, how do you usually respond? Do you distract yourself, vent, or shut down?

----

3. What is the difference between the world's version of peace, which depends on circumstances, and the peace Jesus gives, which lasts no matter what?

----

4. Can you remember a time you felt unexpected peace in the middle of stress? What helped you find it?

----

5. What small habits could you build into your day to create space for God's peace, such as prayer, worship, journaling, or stillness?

In a world that constantly feels loud and busy, **Jesus offers something precious: His peace.** It is not fragile or temporary. It is deep, strong, and unshakable. When life feels out of control, you do not have to fix everything or carry the weight alone.

You can stop. You can breathe. You can rest in His promise. **His peace guards your heart. His calm steadies your soul. His presence reminds you that you are never alone.**

Faith in Action Challenge

Create a "Peace Playlist" with worship songs that help you feel calm and close to God. Play it when anxiety starts to rise and let His presence quiet your heart.

Week 10

I Am Peaceful

"And the peace of God, which transcends all understanding, will guard your hearts and your minds in Christ Jesus."
Philippians 4:7

Have you ever felt like your mind is under attack? Maybe anxious thoughts will not leave you alone. You replay worst-case scenarios, cringe over embarrassing moments, or stress about things that have not even happened yet. You tell yourself to *"just think positively,"* but the worries keep breaking through. You wonder if you will ever feel truly peaceful again.

Here is the truth that can change everything: **God offers you a peace that does not make sense, and that is precisely what makes it so powerful.**

This kind of peace does not come from everything being perfect. It comes from trusting that God is in control, even when life feels out of control. His peace is not fragile or temporary. It is strong and protective, like a fortress guarding your heart and mind. When you give your fears to Him, His peace not only calms your feelings; it also shields your thoughts from being overwhelmed.

Think about it, Paul wrote these words while sitting in prison, unsure of what his future would hold. He had every reason to panic, yet he spoke about a peace that *"transcends understanding."* That is the kind of peace God wants to give you, peace that shows up when life does not make sense, peace that fills your heart when fear tries to take over.

Today, let God's peace stand guard over your thoughts and emotions. Take out your journal or open your notes app and make two simple lists. In the first column, write down the worries or fears that keep looping in your mind. Be specific: school stress, friendships, your future, family tension, anything. Then, next to each one, write these words: **"I am giving this to God."**

Imagine yourself physically handing each worry to Him. You do not have to fix it or figure it out. Let His peace take its place. Then say this truth out loud: **"God's peace guards my heart and mind. I do not have to understand it. I will trust it. I am at peace because He is in control."**

Reflection

1. What fears or worries take up the most space in your mind right now?

----

2. Why do you think Paul describes God's peace as something that transcends understanding? Have you ever felt peace that did not make sense in the moment?

----

3. What does it mean for God's peace to guard your heart and mind? What might it be protecting you from?

----

4. How do you usually handle stress? Do you try to control it, avoid it, or talk it out? How could giving it to God look different?

----

5. What are a few practical ways you can remind yourself during the day that God's peace is already guarding your heart?

True peace is not something you create by fixing your problems or finding all the answers. It comes from releasing control and trusting that **God already has it handled.** His peace is supernatural. It guards your heart like a fortress and protects your thoughts from spinning out of control.

You do not have to hold everything together. You do not have to carry every worry. **God's peace is already covering you.**

So take a breath. Let your heart rest. **You are peaceful because His peace is guarding you.**

Faith in Action Challenge

Each morning this week, start your day by praying, "God, guard my heart and mind with Your peace today." When stress shows up, take a deep breath and whisper, *"Your peace protects me."* Let that reminder calm your spirit and steady your thoughts.

Week 11

I Am Hopeful

"May the God of hope fill you with all joy and peace as you trust in Him, so that you may overflow with hope by the power of the Holy Spirit."
-Romans 15:13

Have you ever felt like giving up? Maybe you have been disappointed so many times that you have stopped believing things can actually get better. Perhaps a friendship fell apart, a dream did not work out, or a struggle will not seem to end. The future feels uncertain and a little scary, and hope can start to feel like something other people have, but not you.

Here is the truth that can reignite your spirit: **God is not just hopeful. He is the God of Hope.** Hope is part of who He is. When you stay close to Him, hope naturally flows into your life. God's hope is not just wishful thinking or "good vibes." It is a confident trust that His plan is good, even when you cannot yet see it.

As you trust Him, He fills you with joy and peace until your heart overflows with hope through the Holy Spirit. That means His hope is so abundant that it spills out of you, encouraging everyone around you.

Think about it. Hope is like light breaking through the darkness. When everything around you says, *"This is impossible,"* hope quietly whispers, *"With God, all things are possible."* God's hope is not tied to how good your circumstances look. It is rooted in His goodness. Even when you cannot see what is next, you can trust that He is already there, preparing something beautiful for you.

Today, let God fill your heart until it overflows with hope. Grab a piece of paper or open your notes app and write yourself a little **"Hope Note."** Start it like this: **"Dear [Your Name], even when things feel hopeless, God..."** Then finish the sentence with truths about who He is and what He has promised. Write about His faithfulness, His plans for your future, or a verse that comforts you. This is not about pretending everything is fine; it is about reminding yourself that your problems are never bigger than His promises.

Now say this out loud: **"God fills me with hope. I trust His plan for my life. Nothing is too difficult when God is by my side."**

Reflection

1. When you think about your future, what emotions come up: excitement, fear, uncertainty, or something else? Why?

----

2. What is the difference between real hope, which trusts God's promises, and optimism, which focuses on thinking positively?

----

3. Can you think of a time when God brought you through something that once seemed hopeless? What did that show you about Him?

----

4. What does it mean to overflow with hope? How can your hope encourage others who are struggling right now?

----

5. What specific promise from God do you need to cling to today? How can you keep it in focus when doubt creeps in?

Hope is not naïve. It is powerful. It helps you take another step when everything inside you wants to give up. Hope reminds you that God's story for your life is not finished yet.

The God of hope does not want to give you just enough to get by. He wants to fill you completely, with joy, with peace, and with an overflowing hope that cannot be shaken by circumstances.

You do not need to see the whole path to trust the One who is guiding you. You do not need to have all the answers to believe He is good.

Hold on to hope. It will not disappoint you.

Faith in Action Challenge

Send a hopeful message or verse to a friend who is going through a tough time. Remind them that God's promises remain true and that brighter days are ahead.

Week 12

I Am Resilient

"We are hard pressed on every side, but not crushed; perplexed, but not in despair; persecuted, but not abandoned; struck down, but not destroyed."
2 Corinthians 4:8–9

Have you ever felt like life keeps knocking you down? Maybe you failed a test you studied hard for, lost a friendship that meant everything, did not make the team, or are dealing with family struggles that feel too heavy to carry. It can feel like you are being hit from every direction, and you are not sure how much more you can take.

Here is the truth that will anchor you: **you are more resilient than you think.** Resilience does not mean pretending you are okay all the time. It means refusing to give up when things get hard. Paul said it best: *pressed but not crushed, confused but not hopeless, knocked down but not destroyed.* Every struggle has a limit, and every battle you face has purpose. You might bend, but you will not break, because God's strength is holding you together.

Think about it. Resilience is not something you are born with; it is something you build. Every challenge you have faced has taught you something. Every time you have cried but still showed up the next day, you grew stronger. Every time you prayed through pain, trusted through confusion, or forgave when it hurt, you became more resilient. You are not just surviving, you are becoming wiser, braver, and more grounded in who God created you to be.

Today, shift how you see your struggles. Think of one setback or challenge you have faced recently. Instead of asking, *"Why is this happening to me?"* try asking, *"What is God teaching me through this?"* Write your answer down. Then say this truth out loud: **"I am re-**

silient. I may be pressed, but I am not crushed. God's strength is making me stronger through this."

Let every challenge become a stepping stone, not a stumbling block.

Reflection

1. What is the biggest challenge you are facing right now, and how has it been affecting your thoughts or emotions?

----

2. Can you think of a time when you got through something difficult? What helped you bounce back?

----

3. When life gets tough, how do you usually respond? Do you withdraw, push through alone, talk to someone, or pray? What might help you handle it better?

----

4. How have your past struggles made you stronger, wiser, or more compassionate?

----

5. What is one small way you can remind yourself of your resilience this week when you feel like giving up?

You are resilient, not because you never fall, but because you always get back up. Every challenge you face is shaping you into someone stronger, kinder, and more confident in God's power.

God has not brought you this far to leave you now. When life presses in from every side, remember that **you are held together by His strength.**

You may be struck down, but you will never be destroyed. **Keep going. Your resilience is proof that God's power is alive in you.**

Faith in Action Challenge

Write the words *"Pressed but not crushed"* somewhere you will see them often; on a sticky note, your mirror, or in your journal. Each time you look at it, thank God for giving you the strength to keep standing.

Week 13

I Am Patient

"But the fruit of the Spirit is love, joy, peace, forbearance, kindness, goodness, faithfulness, gentleness, and self-control. Against such things there is no law."
Galatians 5:22–23

Have you ever felt like you are stuck in the waiting room of life? Maybe you are waiting for your crush to notice you, for your hard work to finally pay off, for your family situation to get better, or for clarity about your future. Waiting can feel exhausting, like everyone else is moving forward while you stand still, watching the clock tick painfully slowly.

Here is the truth you need to remember: **Patience is not just about waiting. It is about how you wait.** Patience is one of the fruits of the Spirit, which means it is evidence that God is growing something beautiful in you. When you choose patience, you are saying, *"I trust God's timing more than my own."* You are choosing peace over panic, hope over frustration, and faith over fear.

Think about it. God is not making you wait to punish you. He is preparing you. Every waiting season is a growing season. The lessons you are learning now are shaping the person you will become later. Patience builds strength, maturity, and character in ways instant answers never could. It teaches you to enjoy the journey rather than race toward the destination. Some of the best blessings in life are worth waiting for.

Today, practice patience as an act of trust. Think about one thing you have been impatiently waiting for. Instead of stressing about when it will happen, pray about it. Write this prayer somewhere you will see it often: **"God, I trust Your timing. While I wait, grow patience in my heart and help me see what You are teach-**

ing me in this season."

Then say this truth out loud: **"I am patient. I trust God's perfect timing. Every season has a purpose."**

Let patience turn your waiting from frustration into expectation.

Reflection

1. What are you waiting for right now, and how does it make you feel: anxious, frustrated, hopeful, or all of the above?

----

2. How do you usually handle waiting? Do you worry, try to take control, or rest in God's timing?

----

3. Can you think of a time when God's timing turned out to be better than yours? What did that teach you?

----

4. What might God be trying to grow in you during this current season of waiting?

----

5. What is one way you can practice patience this week, in a conversation, a situation, or even with yourself?

You are patient, not because waiting is easy, but because you have learned to trust the One who holds your future. God's timing is never late. It is always perfect. While you wait, He is working in your heart, in your circumstances, and in ways you cannot yet see.

Patience is not passive. It is an active choice to believe that every delay has a purpose. Do not rush what God is still preparing.

Embrace where you are, trust His process, and remember that what you are waiting for is already on its way in God's perfect time.

Faith in Action Challenge

Each time you feel impatient this week, take a deep breath and whisper, *"God's timing is perfect."* Let those words remind you that He is working behind the scenes, even when you cannot see it.

Week 14

I Am Faithful

"Let us hold unswervingly to the hope we profess, for He who promised is faithful."
Hebrews 10:23

Have you ever felt like giving up on something or someone? Maybe you started the school year full of excitement and goals, but now you are just tired. Perhaps you are always the one putting in the effort in friendships, even when it feels one-sided. Or maybe life feels messy, unpredictable, and exhausting, and quitting sounds easier than holding on.

Here is the truth that will steady your heart: **faithfulness means showing up, even when it is hard.** It means choosing to stay loyal when walking away would be simpler. It means holding on when others let go and trusting God's promises even when you cannot see the whole picture.

Your faithfulness is not about being perfect or having it all together. It is about reflecting **God's unshakable faithfulness** toward you. He never quits, never breaks His word, and never stops loving you. Because He is faithful, you can learn to be faithful too.

Think about it. Faithfulness builds strength that lasts. When you stay committed to God, your values, your friendships, or your goals, you are creating something solid, something that will not fall apart when life gets tough. Being faithful does not mean you never doubt or struggle. It means you keep showing up anyway. You keep believing. You keep trusting that God is working, even when things do not make sense.

Today, recommit to what matters most. Think of one area in your life where you have been tempted to quit; maybe your faith, a dream, a friendship, or a goal. Write down this declaration:

"I choose faithfulness. Even when it is hard, I will hold on to hope because God is faithful to me."

Then say this out loud: **"I am faithful. I trust God's promises. His loyalty to me makes me loyal in return."**

Let faithfulness be the anchor that keeps you steady when everything else feels uncertain.

Reflection

1. What commitment, relationship, or goal in your life is currently testing your faithfulness?

---

2. What usually makes you want to give up: discouragement, fear, exhaustion, or something else?

---

3. Can you remember a time when God stayed faithful to you even when you felt like giving up? What did you learn from that experience?

---

4. What is one practical way you can show faithfulness this week, to God, to a friend, or to something you have started?

---

5. How does remembering God's faithfulness give you strength to stay consistent and hopeful?

You are faithful, not because you never waver, but because you choose **loyalty over convenience and commitment over comfort.** God's faithfulness toward you never changes, and that same steady strength lives inside you.

When life feels uncertain, when people disappoint you, or when your emotions try to pull you away, remember this: **you can hold on because He is holding you.**

Do not quit on what matters. Keep showing up. Keep trusting. Your faithfulness today is building a foundation that will carry you through every tomorrow.

Faith in Action Challenge

Think of someone who has been a consistent source of encouragement in your life. Send them a note or message to thank them for their faithfulness. It is a small act that reminds you what steady love looks like in action.

Week 15

I Am Creative

"And He has filled him with the Spirit of God, with wisdom, with understanding, with knowledge, and with all kinds of skills—to make artistic designs for work in gold, silver, and bronze, to cut and set stones, to work in wood, and to engage in all kinds of crafts."
Exodus 35:31–32

Have you ever felt like you have nothing special to offer? Maybe you see other people's talents on display: the girl who sings beautifully, the friend who gets straight A's without even trying, or the influencer who seems to have the perfect life, and you wonder, *"What about me?"* It is easy to start believing the lie that you are just ordinary. Not creative. Not talented. Not special.

Here is the truth that changes everything: **you are creative because you are made in the image of a creative God.** Creativity is not just about being artistic or musical. It is about how you think, dream, problem-solve, and express yourself. God has filled you with His Spirit, giving you wisdom, understanding, and unique skills that no one else has in quite the same way. Your creativity is His gift to you, designed to reflect His beauty in the world around you.

Think about it. Creativity shows up in countless ways. Maybe it is how you style an outfit, how you encourage a friend, how you write, dance, organize your space, plan a get-together, or come up with ideas that make people smile. Whatever makes your heart come alive and helps you lose track of time, that is creativity. God placed those passions and abilities in you on purpose. They are not random. They are reminders that you were made to reflect the Creator Himself.

Today, celebrate and use your God-given creativity. Make a list of things you love doing, even if they seem small or unimportant. Drawing, baking, helping others, designing, playing an instrument, and coming up with new ideas all matter. Choose one thing from your list and do it this week, not to impress anyone, but to honor

God and express the creativity He has placed in you.

Then say this out loud: **"I am creative. God has filled me with unique gifts, and I will use them to reflect His beauty and bless others."**

Let your creativity become an act of worship, and a way of saying "Thank You" to the God who made you wonderfully original.

Reflection

1. What activities or interests make you feel the most alive and excited? How might those reflect God's creativity in you?

----

2. Have you ever compared your abilities to someone else's? What would it look like to stop comparing and start celebrating your unique gifts?

----

3. How could you use your creativity this week to encourage someone, share your faith, or make something beautiful?

----

4. What creative dream or idea have you been too afraid to try? What is one small step you could take toward it this week?

----

5. How does using your creativity help you feel closer to God or more like the person He made you to be?

You are creative, not because you have to be the best at something, but because **God intentionally designed you with imagination, ideas, and gifts that are one of a kind.** Your creativity is meant to be shared and celebrated, not hidden or compared.

When you create through words, art, ideas, kindness, or innovation, you mirror the heart of your Creator. Do not let fear or comparison dim your light.

The world needs what only you can bring. Use your gifts boldly, joyfully, and unapologetically, and let your creativity reflect the beauty of the God who made you.

Faith in Action Challenge

Spend time this week creating something that brings you joy. Write, draw, cook, design, or dream. As you do, whisper a quiet prayer of thanksgiving to God for making you creative in your own unique way.

Week 16

I Am Confident

"For the Lord will be at your side and will keep your foot from being snared."
Proverbs 3:26

Have you ever held back because you were afraid of failing or looking foolish? Maybe there is a dream in your heart that you have been too scared to chase because that voice in your head keeps whispering, *"You are not good enough."* Or maybe you avoid speaking up in class, trying out for something new, or sharing your faith because you are afraid of being rejected or judged. Insecurity has a sneaky way of convincing you to play small, stay quiet, and hide your potential.

Here is the truth that sets you free: **confidence is not about believing you can do everything. It is about knowing you do not have to do it alone.** Real confidence comes from knowing that God is with you. When the Lord is at your side, you do not have to have all the answers or be perfectly fearless. You can step forward in faith, try new things, and take risks because His presence gives you strength and His protection keeps you steady.

Think about it. **The Lord is at your side.** Let that sink in for a moment. The Creator of the universe, the One who knows you inside and out and loves you endlessly, is walking beside you. He is not watching from a distance; He is right there, guarding your steps and cheering you on. With Him by your side, what do you really have to fear?

Today, step forward boldly with the confidence God has already given you. Think of one thing you have been too afraid to try, something you have wanted to do, but fear has been holding you back. Write down this truth: **"The Lord is at my side. I do not have to be perfect or fearless. I have to trust Him and take the next step."**

Pray over it, and then take one small action this week toward that goal. It could be signing up for something new, starting a conversation, or simply sharing an idea. As you do, remind yourself:

"I am confident because God is with me. His presence gives me courage to step out and pursue what He has called me to do."

Let your confidence be based on His faithfulness, not on your abilities.

Reflection

1. What dream, goal, or opportunity have you been avoiding because of fear or insecurity? What about it feels scary?

----

2. How does knowing that God is at your side change the way you view challenges or risks?

----

3. Can you remember a time when you acted in faith even though you were afraid, and when you saw God show up for you?

----

4. What would you do differently this week if you truly believed that God's presence makes you capable and courageous?

----

5. How can you encourage a friend who is struggling with confidence to trust that God is with her, too?

You are confident, not because you have it all figured out, but **because the Lord is at your side every single moment.** His presence takes the pressure off being perfect and gives you the courage to be brave.

You do not need to have it all together to take a step of faith. You need to trust the One who walks beside you, guiding, protecting, and empowering you to do what He has called you to do.

Do not let fear make your decisions. Step out boldly. You are never alone, and with God by your side, you can face anything.

Faith in Action Challenge

Write the words *"God is with me"* somewhere you will see them every day; on your mirror, your planner, or your phone lock screen. Each time you see it, take a deep breath and remind yourself that His presence gives you the courage to take your next step.

Week 17

I Am Enough

"But He said, 'My grace is sufficient for you, for My power is made perfect in weakness.' Therefore, I will boast all the more gladly about my weaknesses, so that Christ's power may rest on me."
2 Corinthians 12:9

Have you ever felt like you are just not measuring up? Maybe you scroll through social media and start comparing yourself to everyone else's highlight reels, the perfect selfies, the excellent grades, and flawless friendships. Or maybe you feel crushed by the pressure to always look happy, excel at school, or be everything to everyone. The voice in your head keeps whispering, *"You are not smart enough. Not pretty enough. Not talented enough. Not enough."*

Here is the truth that changes everything: **God's grace is enough for you.** His grace is not partial, limited, or conditional; it is completely sufficient. You do not need to earn it or prove yourself worthy of it. You do not have to hide your struggles or pretend to have it all together. God's grace covers every weakness, insecurity, and flaw. And the best part? It is in those weak moments, when you feel like you have fallen short, that His power shines the brightest.

Think about what Paul is saying in this verse. He actually boasts about his weaknesses. Why? Because when he is weak, Christ's strength shines even more. Your imperfections do not disqualify you; they are invitations for God to step in and show His power. The very places where you feel *"not enough"* are the exact spaces where He wants to pour out His grace.

Today, take a deep breath and receive this truth: **you are enough because God's grace makes you complete.** Grab your journal or open your notes app and write down one area where you often feel *"not enough."* It could be your grades, appearance, friendships, or confidence. Then, right next to it, write this: **"God's grace is sufficient for me here. His power is made perfect in my weakness."**

Say it out loud until it sinks into your heart: **"I am complete in Christ. His grace fills every gap. I am enough because He says I am."**

Let that truth become louder than your inner critic. You do not have to strive to be enough; you already are, in Him.

Reflection

1. What situations or comparisons make you feel like you are "not enough"? Be honest about what triggers those feelings.

----

2. When you feel inadequate, where do you usually turn for comfort: social media, achievements, or other people's approval? How does that make you feel?

----

3. What would change if you truly believed God's grace is sufficient and you do not have to prove your worth?

----

4. Can you recall a time when God showed His strength through your weakness or failure? What did you learn from that?

----

5. What is one practical way you can remind yourself this week that you are complete in Christ when insecurity creeps in?

You are enough, not because you have done enough, achieved enough, or become enough on your own, but because **God's grace is sufficient for you.** His power does not wait for you to be perfect. It meets you right where you are weak.

When you feel like you are falling short, remember that is the very place where His strength shines the brightest. You do not need to prove your worth or earn His love; you already have it.

You are enough, completely, fully, and beautifully because His grace says so.

Faith in Action Challenge

Write the words *"His grace is enough"* on a sticky note, your mirror, or your phone screen. Each time you see it this week, pause and thank God for filling the spaces where you feel weak or unworthy.

Week 18

I Am Unique

"I praise You because I am fearfully and wonderfully made; Your works are wonderful, I know that full well."
Psalm 139:14

Have you ever wished you could be more like someone else? Maybe you scroll through social media and think, *"I wish I had her confidence, her style, her life."* Or perhaps you look around your friend group and feel like everyone else has something special except you. It is tempting to hide the parts of yourself that feel different just to fit in. But here is the truth: **God never created you to blend in.**

God designed you with intention, care, and purpose. You were not mass-produced or randomly assembled. You were fearfully and wonderfully made, crafted with careful thought and loving detail. Your personality, your laugh, your dreams, and even the little quirks you sometimes wish you could change are all part of His masterpiece.

Think about it: there are more than eight billion people in the world, and not one of them has your exact combination of gifts, experiences, or perspective. That is not an accident. It is God's artistry. Your uniqueness is not a flaw to hide; it is a gift to share. The world does not need another copy of someone else; it needs **you**, exactly as God made you.

Today, thank God for making you one of a kind. Create a **"Unique Me"** list in your journal or notes app. Write down at least five things that make you different: your sense of humour, creativity, kindness, boldness, curiosity, or even something quirky you secretly love about yourself. Then, look at your list and say this out loud:

"Thank You, God, for making me unique. I am fearfully and wonderfully made, and I will celebrate who You created me to be."

Let this truth set you free from the pressure to fit in or compare. You do not have to change to be loved. You simply need to be who God made you to be.

Reflection

1. What qualities, interests, or quirks make you unique? What do you love most about how God made you?

----

2. When have you felt pressure to hide who you are to fit in? How did that make you feel inside?

----

3. How would your confidence grow if you fully embraced your individuality instead of comparing yourself to others?

----

4. Can you think of a time when your unique gifts or perspective helped someone else or made a situation better?

----

5. What is one way you can honor God this week by boldly being your authentic self?

You are not a copy. You are an **original masterpiece.** God did not make a mistake when He designed you. Every detail about you carries His signature and purpose. Your uniqueness is His way of saying, *"The world needs you exactly as I made you."*

Stop shrinking back or trying to blend in. Stand tall, be confident, and shine as the one-of-a-kind creation you are. **Your uniqueness is not an accident; it is a reflection of God's creative heart.**

Faith in Action Challenge

This week, use one of your unique gifts to bless someone else. Whether it is writing an encouraging note, sharing your creativity, or simply being a good listener, let your individuality reflect God's love in a way only you can.

Week 19

I Am Generous

"Each of you should give what you have decided in your heart to give, not reluctantly or under compulsion, for God loves a cheerful giver."
2 Corinthians 9:7

Have you ever held back from giving because you felt like you did not have enough? Perhaps you wanted to help a friend but thought you were too busy or did not know what to say. You might have seen a need but felt that what you had to offer wasn't enough to make a difference. Or maybe you have felt pressured to give, and instead of feeling joyful, it just felt draining. In a world that tells you to hold tightly to what is yours, generosity can feel risky.

Here is the truth that transforms everything: **real generosity flows from trusting that God has already given you more than enough.** You give not because your resources are endless, but because you know God's supply never runs out. When you share your time, encouragement, creativity, or energy, you are reflecting His giving heart. God does not want your giving to come from guilt or pressure. He wants it to come from joy. He loves a cheerful giver; someone who gives freely, not because they have to, but because they want to.

Think about it. Even small acts of generosity can have a huge impact: a kind text to a friend who is struggling, sharing a snack, helping someone with homework, volunteering your time, or using your creative talents to brighten someone's day. It is not about how much you give. It is about the love behind it. God delights in a heart that gives cheerfully, no matter how small the gift may seem.

Today, ask God to show you one way you can be generous this week. Write down one thing you have to offer: your time, your words, your creativity, your attention, or even something simple you own. Then pray: **"God, help me to give this cheerfully and freely. Show me who needs what I have to offer, and fill my heart with joy as I share."**

Let God shift your heart from focusing on what you lack to celebrating all that you can give.

Reflection

1. What gifts, talents, or resources has God given you that you can share with others? Think beyond money and consider your time, encouragement, and creativity.

____

____

2. What holds you back from being generous? Is it fear of not having enough, or the fear that your gift will not make a difference?

____

____

3. Can you remember a time when someone's generosity deeply impacted you? What did it teach you about the power of giving?

____

____

4. How does giving to others change your own heart? What have you learned about God through being generous?

____

____

5. What is one specific way you can practice cheerful giving this week, and who might need what you have to offer?

____

____

Generosity is not about having more. It is about trusting that God will provide what you need as you give. When you live with open hands and an open heart, you begin to see just how abundant God's blessings really are.

Even the smallest act of kindness can spark something beautiful. A cheerful word, a thoughtful gesture, or a moment of your time can remind someone that they are seen and loved by God.

You are generous, not because you have everything, but because you know the One who does. Let your giving reflect His heart. **Give freely, give joyfully, and watch how God uses your generosity to change the world around you, one small act of love at a time.**

Faith in Action Challenge

This week, surprise someone with an unexpected act of kindness. Write an encouraging note, share something you love, or offer to help without being asked. Let your generosity reflect God's goodness.

Week 20

I Am Forgiving

"Bear with each other and forgive one another if any of you has a grievance against someone. Forgive as the Lord forgave you."
Colossians 3:13

Have you ever been hurt so badly that you did not want to forgive? Maybe a friend betrayed your trust, and you keep replaying it in your mind. Perhaps someone said something that cut deep, and you still feel that sting every time you think about it. Or maybe you are holding on to anger because forgiveness feels like letting them off the hook, as if forgiving means saying what they did was okay. The truth is, holding on to bitterness feels easier than letting go, but it also keeps you stuck.

Here is the truth that can set you free: **forgiveness is not about excusing what happened; it is about freeing yourself from the weight of it.** When you hold on to resentment, it does not hurt the other person as much as it hurts you. It is like carrying around a heavy backpack full of anger and pain. You end up being the one weighed down. But when you choose to forgive, you are choosing freedom. You are choosing peace. And most importantly, you are choosing to reflect the same forgiveness God shows you every single day.

Think about it. God does not keep a record of your wrongs or hold them against you. He forgives you fully, freely, and completely, no conditions, no grudges. He does not say, *"I will forgive you when you deserve it."* He forgives because that is who He is. And when you choose to forgive others, you are following His example, not because the person deserves it, but because **you deserve the peace that comes from letting go.**

Today, take a brave step toward freedom through forgiveness. Grab your journal or a piece of paper and write down the name of someone you need to forgive. You do not have to send it or tell them; this is between you and God. Write out what happened and how it made you feel. Be honest about your pain. Then write this prayer:

"God, I choose to forgive [name], not because they deserve it, but because You forgave me. Help me release this hurt and experience Your healing in my heart."

Pray those words out loud, and let God begin the process of healing you from the inside out.

Reflection

1. Is there someone you are struggling to forgive right now? What happened, and why is it so hard to let go?

----

2. How has holding on to unforgiveness affected your emotions, thoughts, or peace? What is it costing you to keep carrying it?

----

3. What is the difference between forgiving someone and trusting them again? (Hint: forgiveness brings healing, while trust takes time and healthy boundaries.)

----

4. How does remembering God's forgiveness toward you make it easier to extend forgiveness to others?

----

5. What is one step you can take this week toward forgiveness: praying for the person, journaling your feelings, or asking God for the strength to begin?

Remember, **Forgiveness does not mean pretending it did not hurt.** It does not mean trusting someone again right away or saying what they did was okay. It simply means releasing your hold on the pain and allowing God to heal what has been broken.

When you forgive, you are choosing peace over bitterness, healing over hurt, and freedom over resentment. You are reflecting the heart of God, who forgave you first.

You are forgiving, not because it is easy, but because you are brave enough to let go and trust God with the outcome. **Choose forgiveness today, not for them, but for you.**

Faith in Action Challenge

This week, pray for someone who has hurt you, even if it is still painful. Ask God to bless them and to keep softening your heart as you walk toward forgiveness.

Week 21

I Am Compassionate

"Because of the Lord's great love, we are not consumed, for His compassions never fail. They are new every morning; great is Your faithfulness."
Lamentations 3:22–23

Have you ever been so caught up in your own world that you missed someone else's pain? Maybe a friend was struggling, but you were too distracted to notice. Perhaps you saw someone sitting alone but did not know what to say, so you said nothing. Or maybe you have been so overwhelmed by your own problems that you have not had much space for someone else's. In a fast-paced world full of distractions, it is easy to overlook the quiet needs right in front of you.

Here is the truth that opens your heart: **God's compassion toward you never fails, and He invites you to reflect that same compassion to others.** Every morning, His mercies are brand new. God sees your struggles, your tears, and your worries, and He responds with care. When you take time to see others the way He sees you through empathy, gentleness, and love, you are mirroring His heart.

Think about it. Compassion is not just feeling sorry for someone. It is stepping into their story. It is sitting with a friend in silence when words will not help. It is noticing when someone's smile does not reach their eyes and asking, *"Are you really okay?"* It is choosing to care, even when it costs your time or comfort. Compassion says, *"I see you. You matter. You are not alone."*

Today, ask God to give you eyes to see and a heart that feels. Think of someone in your life who might be struggling; maybe they have been distant, quieter than usual, or seem weighed down. Write their name down and ask God how you can show compassion this week. It could be sending a kind message, sitting with them at lunch, offering to pray for them, or simply listening without trying to fix things.

Pray this: **"God, thank You for Your compassion that never fails. Help me see others the way You see them, and give me the courage to show genuine care and kindness."**

Let His compassion in you become someone else's reminder that they are loved and seen.

Reflection

1. Who in your life might need extra kindness or support right now? What signs have you noticed that they are struggling?

----

2. When you were hurting, what kind of compassion from others meant the most to you?

----

3. What usually stops you from reaching out: busyness, not knowing what to say, or something else?

----

4. How does remembering God's endless compassion toward you help you show more compassion to others?

----

5. What is one specific way you can show compassion this week to someone who needs it?

Compassion is one of the most powerful ways to show God's love. When you take time to notice, listen, and care, you become a reflection of His kindness in a hurting world.

Even the smallest act of compassion, whether it's a listening ear, a hug, or a thoughtful text, can shine light into someone's darkness. You are compassionate because the God who made you is full of compassion.

Let His mercy flow through you today, reminding others that they are seen, valued, and never alone.

Faith in Action Challenge

Reach out to someone who seems distant or discouraged this week. Let them know you care. Send a kind message, ask how they are really doing, or simply be present. Your compassion might be the reminder they need that they are not forgotten.

Week 22

I Am Resourceful

"And my God will meet all your needs according to the riches of His glory in Christ Jesus."
Philippians 4:19

Have you ever felt stuck, like you do not have what it takes to handle what is in front of you? Maybe you are staring at a problem at school and have no clue where to start. You might have a dream, but you do not have the money, connections, or confidence to make it happen. Or maybe you feel overwhelmed, like the challenges in front of you are way bigger than your abilities.

Here is the truth that empowers you: **God promises to meet all your needs, and He has already equipped you with more than you think.** You might not have everything you want, but you have everything you need for the season you are in right now. God has given you creativity, determination, and the ability to think differently. Being resourceful is not about having endless supplies. It is about trusting that God's provision, combined with your willingness, equals more than enough.

Think about it. Some of the most incredible ideas come from people who had little to start with. When things do not come easily, you learn to think creatively and find new ways forward. Every time you solve a problem, stretch your imagination, or ask God for wisdom, you are proving that resourcefulness is not about what is in your hands; it is about **Who is in your heart.**

Today, take on your challenges with confidence in God's provision and your own resourcefulness. Think of one problem or goal that has been stressing you out and write it down. Then list everything you already have that can help: your skills, time, ideas, support from others, and past experiences. You will be surprised by how much God has already placed in your life.

Then pray this: **"God, thank You for providing everything I need. Help me use what I have wisely, think creatively, and trust You to fill in what I lack."**

Step forward knowing you are not limited; you are equipped.

Reflection

1. What challenges are you facing right now that require resourcefulness? How have you handled similar situations before?

----

2. When you feel stuck, what is your first reaction: to give up, panic, ask for help, or start problem-solving?

----

3. How does knowing that God will meet all your needs give you courage to take on challenging situations?

----

4. What gifts, skills, or experiences has God given you that you can use more creatively?

----

5. What is one step you can take this week to move forward in faith, trusting both your God-given resourcefulness and His provision?

You are more capable than you realize. God has already given you the creativity, intelligence, and determination you need to face challenges with confidence.

He does not always hand you everything at once, but He always provides what you need when you need it. Your resourcefulness reflects His abundance at work in your life.

You are resourceful because you are connected to a God who never runs out of ideas, power, or provision. Do not focus on what is missing. Look at what is already in your hands and trust that He will supply the rest.

Faith in Action Challenge

This week, find one creative way to solve a problem or bless someone using what you already have. Ask God to help you see possibilities where others see limits, and thank Him for making you capable and resourceful.

Week 23

I Am Thoughtful

"Let each of you look not only to his own interests but also to the interests of others."
Philippians 2:4

Have you ever been so focused on your own world that you missed what someone else was going through? Maybe you were sharing your struggles with a friend, but forgot to ask how they were doing. Perhaps you said something without thinking and only later realized your words hurt more than you intended. It is not that you do not care; you just get caught up in your own plans, emotions, or to-do list. In a world that constantly tells you to *"focus on yourself,"* it is easy to forget to look up and notice others.

Here is the truth that transforms your relationships: **thoughtfulness is love in action.** It is paying attention to how your words and actions affect others and choosing to respond with care. Being thoughtful does not mean being perfect; it means being intentional. It means pausing before speaking, noticing when someone looks sad, or doing something kind without being asked. Thoughtfulness is remembering what matters to people, showing up when they need support, and caring enough to listen.

Think about it: the most meaningful friendships are built on small moments of thoughtfulness. When someone takes the time to really listen, check in, or do something kind, it makes you feel seen and valued. Your thoughtfulness has that same power; it can brighten someone's day, strengthen a friendship, or remind someone that they matter. The best part is that it costs nothing and requires nothing significant. It just takes a heart that notices and cares.

Today, practice intentional thoughtfulness toward someone in your life. Think of one person: a friend, a family member, a teacher, or someone who has been quiet lately. Ask yourself: "What might they need right now? Are they stressed, celebrating, or going through something challenging?" Write down one thoughtful action you can take: sending a kind text, offering help, writing a note, giving a compliment, or simply spending time with them.

Then pray this: **"God, help me to be mindful of others and see beyond my own needs. Give me a heart that notices, listens, and loves through thoughtful actions."**

Let your thoughtfulness reflect God's gentle care toward you.

Reflection

1. When was the last time someone did something thoughtful for you? What made it meaningful?

2. Are there relationships in your life where you have been more focused on yourself than on the other person? How could being more thoughtful strengthen those connections?

3. What keeps you from being thoughtful: busyness, forgetfulness, fear, or thinking it is not that important?

4. How can you balance caring for yourself while also being attentive to others' needs? (Remember, being thoughtful does not mean neglecting yourself.)

5. What is one habit you can build this week to help you become

more thoughtful, like setting reminders to check in with people, keeping track of important dates, or pausing before you speak?

Thoughtfulness is love made visible through small, intentional acts of kindness. When you take time to notice and care for others, you mirror God's tender love in a world that often rushes past people's pain.

Your words, attention, and actions have the power to comfort, encourage, and remind someone that they are not alone. You are thoughtful, not because you have it all together, but because you are choosing to see others with God's eyes.

In a distracted, self-focused world, your thoughtfulness shines like light. Let it remind others that they are seen, valued, and deeply loved.

Faith in Action Challenge

This week, make thoughtfulness your mission. Each morning, ask God to show you one person who needs a little extra kindness or encouragement that day. Then act on it; send a message, write a note, share a compliment, or simply take time to listen.

Week 24

I Am Capable

"Now go; I will help you speak and will teach you what to say."
Exodus 4:12

Have you ever doubted whether you could do something mean-ingful? Maybe you are facing a big test, a performance, or a tough conversation and feel entirely unprepared. Maybe there is a dream in your heart that feels way too big for someone like you. Or perhaps you have failed before and are now scared to even try again. When life feels overwhelming, it is easy to focus on what you *cannot* do rather than on what you *can*.

Here is the truth that changes everything: **God has already equipped you with what you need, and He promises to help you when you need it most.** You are more capable than you think. The same God who told Moses, "I will help you speak and will teach you what to say," is the same God who walks beside you through every challenge. He never calls you to do something without also giving you the strength, wisdom, and courage to do it.

Think about it: even Moses felt unqualified when God called him to lead. He argued with God, made excuses, and focused on his weaknesses. But God did not back down. He reminded Moses that He would be with him and give him the words and tools he need-ed. That is what God does for you, too. Your capability is not about your confidence or your talent; it is about **His power working through you.** When you take that first step of faith, God meets you there with guidance, wisdom, and the help you need to keep going.

Today, choose to trust in your God-given capabilities instead of your fears. Think of one goal or challenge you have been avoiding because of self-doubt. Maybe it is trying something new, having a difficult conversation, or starting something that scares you. Write down this prayer: **"God, I feel incapable, but I trust that You have equipped me and will help me. I am going to take one**

step forward in faith."

Then take one small, practical step toward that goal. You do not have to have it all figured out; you just need to start. As you move forward, say this out loud: **"I am capable because God has equipped me and promises to help me. I will trust His guidance and step forward with confidence."**

Reflection

1. What talents or abilities make you feel most capable and confident? How have you seen God use them in your life?

----

2. What areas make you feel least capable? What fears or doubts hold you back from stepping out?

----

3. Can you remember a time when you felt completely unprepared but God helped you anyway? What did that teach you about His faithfulness?

----

4. How does knowing that God promises to equip and guide you change the way you approach challenges?

----

5. What is one achievable goal you can work toward this week, trusting that God will give you what you need along the way?

You are capable of more than you realize. God did not create you to live small or afraid. He made you with purpose, potential, and everything you need to succeed through His strength.

Your capability is not limited to what you can do on your own. It includes everything God can do through you when you trust Him.

Stop letting fear or insecurity hold you back. Step forward with confidence, knowing that the One who calls you also equips you.

You are capable, not because you are perfect, but because God is with you, guiding and empowering you every step of the way.

Faith in Action Challenge

This week, take one small step toward something that has been holding you back. It could be speaking up when you usually stay quiet, trying something new that scares you, or finally starting the project you have been putting off. Let your action be a reminder that you are capable through God's strength and that every step forward, no matter how small, is an act of faith.

Week 25

I Am Valuable

"So do not be afraid; you are worth more than many sparrows."
Matthew 10:31

Have you ever measured your worth by what others think of you? Maybe you catch yourself checking how many likes your posts get or how often someone texts you back. Maybe you tie your worth to your grades, how well you perform, or whether people notice your efforts. When you fall short, get overlooked, or face rejection, it is easy to feel like you are just not enough. When your sense of value depends on things that constantly change, your confidence will always feel shaky.

Here is the truth that anchors your identity: **your worth is not determined by popularity, success, or other people's approval. It is defined by God's unchanging love for you.** Jesus said you are worth more than many sparrows, and He meant it. God does not love you because of what you do. He loves you because of who you are: His creation, His daughter, His treasure. Your value is not something you earn. It is something you were born with. Nothing you achieve can increase it, and nothing you fail at can decrease it.

Think about it. God does not measure your worth by your GPA, your social circle, or your reflection in the mirror. He looks at you with pure love and says, "You are Mine." You cannot work harder to make Him love you more, and you cannot mess up badly enough for Him to love you less. Your value is fixed, secure, steady, and forever. When you understand that truth, you stop chasing approval and start walking in peace.

Let God's truth define your worth today. Write out this declaration and keep it somewhere you will see often: on your mirror, in your phone notes, or in your Bible:

"I am valuable because God says I am. My worth does not de-

pend on what I achieve, how I look, or what others think of me. I am loved unconditionally, chosen intentionally, and worth more than many sparrows."

Every time you are tempted to question your worth, come back to that truth. Then pray:

"God, thank You for giving me unchanging value. Help me see myself the way You see me: worthy, loved, and enough. I choose to find my worth in You alone."

Reflection

1. What things do you usually rely on to feel valuable: social media, grades, compliments, achievements, or relationships?

2. How does your confidence shift when those things do not go the way you want?

3. What would change in your life if you genuinely believed your worth was permanent and unshakable in God?

4. Can you remember a time you felt completely loved just for being you, not for what you did? What did that moment teach you?

5. What is one simple way you can remind yourself this week that your worth comes from God, not the world?

You are valuable, not because of what you do, but because of who you belong to. Your worth does not rise and fall with people's opinions, accomplishments, or mistakes. It is anchored in the heart of the God who made you and calls you priceless.

Stop chasing the approval of people who cannot give you the lasting affirmation your heart longs for. You are already enough. You are already loved. You are already valuable.

God's opinion of you is final, and He says you are worth everything. Let that truth be your foundation as you walk confidently into every day, knowing your value is unshakable, unchanging, and undeniable.

Faith in Action Challenge

This week, take time each morning to remind yourself, *"I am valuable because God made me and loves me."* Look for one way to live from that truth; whether it is encouraging someone else, speaking kindly to yourself, or choosing peace instead of comparison. Let every action reflect the confidence that your worth comes from God alone.

Week 26

I Am Cherished

"The Lord your God is in your midst, a mighty one who will save; He will rejoice over you with gladness; He will quiet you by His love; He will exult over you with loud singing."
Zephaniah 3:17

Have you ever felt invisible or overlooked? Maybe your friends forgot to include you in their plans. Maybe your efforts went unnoticed, or you feel like you are always the one cheering for others while no one notices you. It hurts to feel unseen, like you are fading into the background while everyone else shines.

Here is the truth that will completely change your perspective: **the God of the universe rejoices over you with gladness and sings over you with love.** Think about that for a moment. The same God who spoke the stars into existence and painted sunsets across the sky looks at you and smiles. He does not just love you in a general sense; He delights in you personally. He rejoices over your life, celebrates your uniqueness, and quiets your worries with His tender love. You are not just known, you are cherished.

Picture this: when you feel anxious, God's love calms your heart. When you feel forgotten, He is singing over you with joy. When you doubt your worth, His voice reminds you that you are treasured beyond measure. You are not one of many; you are the one He adores. You are not an afterthought in His creation; you are the reason He smiles.

Today, let this truth sink deep into your soul: you are cherished by God Himself. Find a quiet moment, and close your eyes. Imagine God looking at you, not with disappointment or frustration, but with delight. He is rejoicing over you with gladness and singing songs of love over your life. Write this truth somewhere you will see it often: **"God rejoices over me with gladness. I am cherished."**

Then say it out loud until you believe it: **"I am cherished by the Creator of the universe. He delights in me and sings over me with joy."**

Let that truth shape how you see yourself today.

Reflection

1. When was the last time you felt overlooked or unimportant? How did it make you feel?

----

2. How does it feel to know that God does not just love you, but actually rejoices over you with singing and delight?

----

3. What would change about the way you see yourself if you genuinely believed you are deeply cherished by God?

----

4. Can you think of a moment when you felt God's love quiet your worries or fears? What did that feel like?

----

5. Who in your life might need to be reminded that they are cherished? How can you show that to them this week?

You are not invisible. You are not forgotten. You are not insignificant. The mighty God who saves is in your midst, celebrating you, loving you, and singing over you with joy.

When the world makes you feel small or unimportant, remember this. The Creator of the universe delights in you. His love quiets your anxious heart, His joy surrounds you, and His song declares your worth.

You are seen. You are known. And you are cherished—deeply, completely, and eternally.

Faith in Action Challenge

This week, take time each day to thank God for the ways He shows His love to you through people, nature, or simple moments of joy. Write down three ways you have felt His love and choose one way to reflect that same love to someone else. As you do, remember that being cherished by God empowers you to love others deeply, too.

Week 27

I Am Healthy

"Dear friend, I hope all is well with you and that you are as healthy in body as you are strong in spirit."
3 John 1:2

Have you ever felt like you are running on empty? Maybe you have been staying up too late scrolling through your phone, skipping meals because you are too busy, or pushing yourself so hard that you cannot remember the last time you truly rested. Life gets overwhelming, and when it does, it is easy to put yourself last.

Here is the truth that might surprise you: **God cares about every part of you; your body, your mind, and your spirit.** He did not just create your soul; He designed your entire being with love and intention. When you take care of your physical, emotional, and spiritual health, you are not being selfish; you are honouring the gift of life He has given you. Taking care of yourself is one of the most loving ways to worship God.

Think about it: you cannot pour from an empty cup. When you are exhausted, overwhelmed, or drained, it is hard to show up fully for others or even for yourself. God wants you to flourish in every area of your life. Eating well, moving your body, and getting enough rest help you stay strong. Setting boundaries, taking breaks, and processing your emotions help your mind stay clear and peaceful. And spending time with God through prayer, Scripture, or worship keeps your spirit grounded and renewed. Every part of you is connected, and every part matters to Him.

Today, remember this truth. God wants you to be healthy and whole, body, mind, and spirit. Take a few minutes to check in with yourself.

• **Body:** Are you getting enough rest and fuel?

• **Mind:** Are you caring for your thoughts and emotions in healthy ways?

• **Spirit:** Are you staying connected to God?

Choose one area that needs attention and commit to a small, simple change this week, like going to bed earlier, journaling your thoughts, or spending ten quiet minutes with God each morning. Write this down and believe it: **"God wants me to flourish in body, mind, and spirit. I will honor the gift of life by caring for myself."**

Say it out loud: **"I am healthy; body, mind, and spirit, because God designed me to thrive."**

Reflection

1. Which area of physical, mental, or spiritual health do you tend to neglect most? Why do you think that is?

----

2. What habits in your daily life help you feel your best? Which habits leave you feeling drained or disconnected?

----

3. How does taking care of your body and mind help you grow stronger in your relationship with God?

----

4. What boundaries or changes could you make this week to protect your well-being?

----

5. How might caring for your health help you love and serve others more effectively?

Being healthy is not about chasing perfection or meeting unrealistic standards. It is about living in balance and gratitude. God designed you with purpose, and He wants every part of you to thrive. When you rest, move, eat well, and spend time with Him, you are saying "Thank You" for the incredible body, mind, and spirit He has given you.

You do not have to overhaul your whole life overnight. Start small. Take one step toward caring for yourself with kindness and intention, and trust that God will meet you there. You are not just surviving, you are meant to flourish.

Faith in Action Challenge

This week, focus on one way to care for your health as an act of worship, whether it is resting well, taking a walk, journaling, or spending quiet time with God. Be intentional about nourishing your body, mind, and spirit. As you do, thank Him for creating you so wonderfully and for giving you the strength to live fully and well.

Week 28

I Am Healed

"But he was pierced for our transgressions, he was crushed for our iniquities; the punishment that brought us peace was on him, and by his wounds we are healed."
Isaiah 53:5

Have you ever felt broken beyond repair? Maybe you are carrying pain from something that happened in your past, or you are dealing with hurt that feels too heavy to let go of. Perhaps you have been wounded by someone's words, struggling with grief, anxiety, or scars that never seem to fade. You might even wonder if you will ever feel whole again.

Here is the truth that offers incredible hope: **Jesus' sacrifice did not just bring forgiveness; it brought healing.** When He suffered on the cross, He carried your pain, your heartbreak, and your struggles. His wounds opened the way for your restoration: body, mind, heart, and soul. No matter what kind of hurt you are facing, His healing power is already at work in your life.

Think about that for a moment: Jesus endured piercing pain and crushing sorrow so that you could have peace. The same power that raised Him from the dead is alive in you, healing what is broken and bringing light to the dark places of your story. Healing may not happen instantly or look precisely the way you expect. Still, it is real, and it is happening; sometimes quietly, sometimes slowly, but always faithfully.

Today, embrace this life-changing truth: through Jesus, you are being healed. Take a few minutes to be honest with God. Think about one area where you are hurting: your heart, your thoughts, your past, or even your body. Do not hide it or downplay it. Write a prayer in your journal that begins, **"Jesus, by Your wounds I am**

healed. I bring You [specific area] and ask You to restore me fully."

Then say this aloud: **"I am not defined by my brokenness. Jesus' sacrifice brings healing to every wounded part of me. I am being restored."**

Let His peace begin to settle in your soul as you trust Him with what hurts most.

Reflection

1. What is one area of your life that feels broken or in need of healing right now? Have you honestly talked to God about it?

----

2. When you think about being healed, what does that look and feel like for you?

----

3. Have you ever seen God bring healing, physical, emotional, or spiritual, in your life? What did that teach you about His love?

----

4. What fears or doubts make it hard to believe that complete healing is possible?

----

5. Who can you open up to about your healing journey: a trusted friend, parent, counselor, or youth leader?

You do not have to carry your pain alone or believe the lie that you are too broken to be made whole. Jesus' wounds are proof that there is no hurt He cannot heal and no scar He cannot redeem. Healing is often a process, not a quick fix, but every step forward is part of God's restoration story for your life.

You are not defined by what has been done to you or what has been broken inside you. You are defined by the One who is making you whole. Take a deep breath and trust that healing, real, lasting, soul-deep, is not only possible; it is already in motion.

You are healed, you are being restored, and you are loved beyond measure.

Faith in Action Challenge

This week, choose one small way to let healing take root. Write a prayer of surrender, forgive someone, or spend quiet time with God reflecting on His love. Each time you feel pain or doubt, whisper, *"By His wounds, I am healed."* Trust that even in the waiting, God is working to make you whole.

Week 29

I Am Thriving

"That person is like a tree planted by streams of water, which yields its fruit in season and whose leaf does not wither—whatever they do prospers."
Psalm 1:3

Have you ever felt like you are just barely getting through each day? Maybe you are stuck in routine: wake up, go to school, scroll through your phone, repeat, without feeling truly alive. Perhaps your faith feels distant, or it seems like everyone else is growing, succeeding, and shining while you are just trying to keep your head above water. You wonder if thriving is even possible for you.

Here is the truth that changes everything: **God did not create you to survive; He created you to thrive.** Like a tree planted by streams of living water, God designed you to flourish, to grow, and to bear fruit that blesses others. Thriving does not depend on having perfect circumstances or a problem-free life. It depends on being rooted in the One who gives life, God Himself.

Think about it. A thriving tree is not strong because it avoids storms but because its roots run deep. The same is true for you. When you stay connected to God through prayer, worship, and His Word, you develop spiritual roots that keep you steady in every season. Even when life feels dry or difficult, His living water sustains you. And as you grow in His presence, fruit begins to appear: peace, joy, kindness, wisdom, and strength. These are not things you have to force; they naturally grow when you are rooted in Him.

Today, remind yourself of this truth: you are meant to thrive, not just survive. Take an honest look at your spiritual roots. Are you staying connected to God, or have you been running on empty? Choose one simple way to draw closer to Him this week. Maybe it is reading a short devotional before bed, spending time in prayer outside, or listening to worship music instead of your usual play-list.

Write this declaration somewhere you will see it every day: **"I am like a tree planted by streams of water. I will bear fruit in season and prosper in all I do because I am rooted in God."**

Say it out loud: **"I am thriving because I am rooted in God's love and nourished by His presence."**

Reflection

1. What areas of your life feel the most alive right now? What is helping you thrive there?

----

2. Where do you feel stuck, drained, or spiritually dry? What might be pulling you away from your source of strength?

----

3. What habits help you feel closest to God and most at peace? How can you make space for more of those this week?

----

4. How do you usually respond during hard seasons: by withdrawing, doubting, or leaning deeper into your faith?

----

5. What would thriving look like for you in this season at school, in friendships, and in your relationship with God?

Thriving does not mean your life is perfect. It means you are growing even when things are not. Just like a strong tree faces both sunshine and storms, you will face challenges too. But when your roots are deep in God's love, you will not wither. You will stand firm, keep growing, and bear fruit in the right season.

God's desire is for you to live fully; to wake up each day connected to Him, strong in faith, and confident in who you are. Keep watering your roots with His Word. Keep reaching toward His light. Keep trusting His timing. When your life is planted in God, you are not just surviving; you are thriving.

Faith in Action Challenge

This week, spend time doing something that helps your faith grow stronger. Read a Psalm each day, take a quiet walk, and pray, or journal what you are grateful for. Ask God to show you one "root" that needs watering, and take one intentional step to nourish it. Remember, thriving starts with staying close to Him.

Week 30

I Am Courageous

"Have I not commanded you? Be strong and courageous. Do not be afraid; do not be discouraged, for the Lord your God will be with you wherever you go."
Joshua 1:9

Have you ever let fear stop you from doing something you knew you should do? Maybe you stayed quiet when you wanted to speak up, avoided trying something new because you were afraid of failing, or let anxiety hold you back from stepping into something exciting. Fear can make us play small, convincing us to stay safe rather than step out in faith.

Here is the truth that will empower you. **Courage is not the absence of fear; it is moving forward in faith despite it**. When God commands you to be strong and courageous, He is not expecting you to have it all together or never feel afraid. He is reminding you that you are not alone. His presence goes with you wherever you go. You do not have to be fearless; you have to be faithful.

Think about what God told Joshua. He was about to lead an entire nation into unknown territory, an intimidating task that required tremendous bravery. But God did not say, "Do not worry; nothing difficult will happen." He said, "Do not be afraid, for I am with you." That is the key to courage, knowing that wherever you go, God goes too. His strength, His power, and His peace are right beside you, giving you the boldness to face what feels impossible.

Today, take a deep breath and step into this truth: **I am courageous because God is with me.** Think of one thing you have been avoiding because of fear: a conversation, a dream, an opportunity, or even a step of obedience. Write it down, and next to it, write: **God is with me in this. I will be strong and courageous.**

Pray and ask God to give you peace and confidence to take one small step this week toward facing that fear. Then say this out loud until it feels true: **"I am courageous. I will not be afraid or discouraged, because the Lord my God is with me wherever I go."**

Let His presence fill you with strength and remind you that you are never facing anything alone.

Reflection

1. What is one fear that has been holding you back lately? What would it look like to face it with courage this week?

----

2. When you feel afraid, how do you usually respond: freeze, avoid, or push through? How does that affect your faith?

----

3. Can you remember a time when you acted courageously even though you were scared? How did God show up for you in that moment?

----

4. What would change in your life if you genuinely believed that God's presence goes with you everywhere you go?

----

5. Who in your life inspires you with their courage? What can you learn from their example?

Being courageous does not mean you will never feel afraid. It means you choose faith over fear every single time. God has not called you to live small or safe; He has called you to step boldly into the life He has designed for you. And the best part is, you never have to do it alone. His presence walks beside you, His Spirit empowers you, and His love covers you wherever you go.

So take that step. Speak that truth. Chase that dream. Even if your knees shake and your heart pounds, move forward knowing the Lord your God is with you. **You are courageous, not because you are fearless, but because you are never alone.**

Faith in Action Challenge

This week, face one fear you have been avoiding, big or small. Pray for courage, take a deep breath, and take one brave step forward. Each time fear tries to hold you back, remind yourself, *"God is with me wherever I go,"* and let His presence strengthen your heart.

Week 31

I Am Growing

"But grow in the grace and knowledge of our Lord and Savior Jesus Christ. To him be glory both now and forever! Amen."
2 Peter 3:18

Have you ever felt frustrated with yourself for not being "there" yet? Maybe you are comparing your progress to someone who seems more confident, more spiritual, or more put-together. Perhaps you have made the same mistake for what feels like the hundredth time, and you are tired of feeling stuck. You wonder if you are actually growing or just standing still.

Here is the truth that can shift your whole perspective: **growth is not about perfection, it is about progress.** God is not asking you to have everything figured out. He is inviting you to keep walking with Him, learning, and becoming more like Jesus one step at a time. Growth takes time, and it is often slow and steady. Even when you cannot see it, God is working beneath the surface, shaping your heart and strengthening your faith.

Think about what Peter is saying: *"Grow in the grace and knowledge of Jesus."* That means, your growth happens in two ways: by experiencing God's grace more deeply and by getting to know Jesus more personally. Every season, whether joyful or painful, is part of that growth. When you fail, you grow in grace. When you succeed, you grow in gratitude. When you face challenges, you grow in faith. Nothing is wasted. God uses every moment to develop your character, deepen your wisdom, and draw you closer to Him.

Today, embrace this freeing truth: **you are growing, and that is precisely where God wants you to be.** Take a moment to reflect on your journey. Look back over the last few months or even the past year. Write down one way you have grown; it could be in your patience, faith, friendships, confidence, or understanding of yourself. Then write down one area where you want to keep growing.

Say this out loud with confidence: **"I am not the same person I was yesterday. I am growing in grace and knowledge of Jesus, and every experience is shaping me for the better."**

Even if you are still a work in progress, celebrate how far you have come, because that is what growth is all about.

Reflection

1. What is one lesson you have learned recently from a mistake, challenge, or success that has helped you grow?

---

2. Where do you tend to be hardest on yourself for not growing fast enough? How can you extend more grace in that area?

---

3. How have you seen yourself change over the past year in your faith, confidence, or relationships?

---

4. What is one area where you feel stuck right now? What small step could you take this week toward growth?

---

5. How can you celebrate your progress instead of focusing only on how far you still have to go?

You are not meant to stay the same; you are meant to grow. Every day offers new chances to learn, change, and become more of who God created you to be. Your growth journey will not look like anyone else's, and that is okay. Even when it feels slow, God is faithfully transforming you from the inside out.

Do not rush the process or compare your timeline to someone else's. Keep showing up. Keep learning. Keep letting God shape your heart. **You are growing in grace, growing in strength, and growing into the beautiful, confident, faith-filled woman He designed you to become.**

Faith in Action Challenge

Take five minutes this week to journal three ways you have grown in the past year and thank God for each one. Then write one area where you want to keep growing and ask Him for wisdom and patience in that process. Growth happens one small step at a time, so take yours with confidence.

Week 32

I Am Learning

"Let the wise hear and increase in learning, and the one who understands obtain guidance."
Proverbs 1:5

Have you ever felt like you already know enough? Maybe you have zoned out in class, brushed off advice from someone who cares about you, or stopped asking questions because you felt like you had it all figured out. Or maybe the opposite, you feel overwhelmed by how much you don't know and wonder if you will ever understand how to handle life.

Here is the truth that opens up endless possibilities: **being willing to learn is one of the wisest and most beautiful things you can do.** Every single day is full of lessons about yourself, others, the world, and God. When you approach life with curiosity rather than pride, and humility rather than fear, you position yourself to grow in wisdom and understanding. God loves a teachable heart. He is always ready to guide you, but He can only teach you if you are willing to listen.

Think about what this verse reveals: even the wise keep learning. Wisdom is not about knowing it all; it is about realizing there is always more to discover. Whether you are figuring out algebra, learning how to be a better friend, understanding your emotions, or growing in your faith, every lesson matters. God uses everything: Scripture, experiences, people, and even your mistakes to teach you and shape you. The question is, are you paying attention?

Today, take on this mindset: **I am a learner, and every day teaches me something valuable.** Think about your attitude toward learning lately. Have you been open and curious, or distracted and resistant? Ask God to be your teacher today. Pay attention to what

He might want to show you through a conversation, a verse, a challenge, or a quiet moment.

At the end of the day, write down one thing you learned and how it changed your perspective. Then say this truth out loud: **"I am a learner. I will approach life with an open mind and heart, seeking wisdom and guidance from God in everything I do."**

Reflection

1. What is one new thing you have learned recently about yourself, someone else, or God? How did it change your perspective?

----

2. In what areas of your life do you tend to think you already know everything? What might God be trying to teach you there?

----

3. Who is someone in your life who teaches you valuable lessons: a parent, friend, teacher, or youth leader? How can you learn from them more intentionally?

----

4. When has God taught you something surprising or powerful through a challenging experience or mistake?

----

5. How can you invite God to be your teacher in everyday moments, at school, with friends, at home, or when you are struggling?

Never stop learning. The moment you think you have arrived is the moment you stop growing. God designed your entire life as a classroom full of opportunities to gain wisdom, build strength, and deepen your understanding of His truth.

Stay curious. Ask questions. Listen well. Be open to correction and willing to try again. Even when lessons come through mistakes or disappointment, God is still teaching you something good. **Every day you learn, you grow a little more into the person He created you to be.** Keep learning. Keep growing. And keep your heart open to the lessons God is writing into your story.

Faith in Action Challenge

This week, ask God to show you one lesson He wants you to learn through a challenge, a person, or a Scripture. Write it down and reflect on how it applies to your life. Stay open, curious, and humble, trusting that every new lesson is shaping your heart for something greater.

Week 33

I Am Inspired

"But it is the spirit in a person, the breath of the Almighty, that gives them understanding."
Job 32:8

Have you ever felt creatively stuck or completely unmotivated? Maybe you have lost excitement for something you used to love. Or perhaps you have been feeling tired, bored, or simply wondering where your spark went. You scroll through social media and see other people living out their passions, and you can't help but think, *what happened to mine?*

Here is the truth that can reignite your fire: **the same Spirit that breathed life into creation lives inside you.** That means you have access to divine inspiration, creativity, hope, and purpose flowing straight from God Himself. When you feel stuck or uninspired, it doesn't mean you have failed; it simply means you need to reconnect with your Source. God's Spirit is always present, ready to breathe fresh life into your heart and remind you why He made you the way He did.

Think about what this verse says: *"The breath of the Almighty gives understanding."* That breath, the Holy Spirit, is constantly at work in you. He sparks new ideas, stirs up passion for your gifts, and helps you see your life with a fresh perspective. Inspiration doesn't **always** appear in a flash; sometimes it grows quietly as you spend time with God, listen to worship music, journal your prayers, or take a walk and talk with Him. He is the ultimate Creator, and He has planted that same creative Spirit in you.

Today, remind yourself of this truth: **I am inspired by the Spirit of God who lives in me.** Think about one dream, project, or passion that has lost its spark. Bring it to God. Ask the Holy Spirit to breathe new life into it and show you what to do next. Then take one small step forward, open your notebook, plan your next move, or thank God for the new vision.

Say this out loud until you believe it: **"The Spirit of the Almighty gives me understanding and inspiration. I am filled with creativity, hope, and passion because God's breath is within me."**

Reflection

1. When do you feel most inspired and alive? What tends to spark that feeling for you: people, places, music, or time with God?

----

2. What dream or passion have you been neglecting lately? What has been holding you back from pursuing it?

----

3. How does spending time with God affect your creativity, motivation, or sense of purpose?

----

4. Who in your life inspires you by the way they live out their faith or creativity? What can you learn from their example?

----

5. How can you use your inspiration to encourage or uplift someone else this week, through art, words, kindness, or simply showing up for them?

You were never meant to live an uninspired life. The Creator of the universe breathed His Spirit into you, filling you with creativity, purpose, and passion that no one else can replicate. When you start to feel stuck or empty, don't panic. Reconnect with the Source. Spend time in God's presence and let His Spirit refresh your heart and renew your ideas.

Don't let fear, comparison, or doubt dim your light. The dreams inside you are not random; they are part of God's design for your life. So take a deep breath, lift your eyes, and step into the inspiration that comes from knowing the Spirit of God is alive and working in you. **You are inspired because His breath is your spark.**

Faith in Action Challenge

This week, spend a few minutes each day in quiet time with God, whether through journaling, prayer, or listening to worship music. Ask Him to reignite a dream or passion that has grown dim and give you one creative way to use it for His glory. Let His Spirit breathe fresh inspiration into your heart.

Week 34

I Am Supported

"God is our refuge and strength, an ever-present help in trouble."
Psalm 46:1

Have you ever felt utterly alone in what you are going through? Maybe you are facing something hard and don't know who to talk to. Perhaps you feel like no one truly understands your pain, or you have been carrying worries that feel too heavy to share. When life gets difficult, loneliness can make everything feel even heavier.

Here is the truth that will anchor your heart: **you are never alone.** God is not watching your life from far away. He is right beside you; an ever-present help in every moment of trouble. He is your safe place when everything feels chaotic and your strength when you feel weak or weary. His support is not something you have to earn or chase after. It is already here, always available, and more than enough.

Think about what this verse promises: God is your refuge and strength. That means you can run to Him whenever you feel afraid, overwhelmed, or unsure. You don't have to hide your emotions or pretend you are fine. He welcomes your honesty, your tears, and your questions. And when you have nothing left to give, His strength carries you. Even in your loneliest moments, He is whispering, *"I'm here. I've got you."*

Today, let this truth settle deep in your heart: *I am fully supported by God, who is always with me.* Take a moment to think about what feels heavy right now. Instead of carrying it by yourself, bring it to God. Write a simple, honest prayer telling Him what has been weighing on your heart and ask Him to give you strength. Then reach out to one person you trust: a friend, parent, youth leader, or counselor, and let them walk with you.

Speak this truth out loud over your situation: **"God is my refuge and strength. He is with me in this moment. I am not alone, I am fully supported."**

Reflection

1. What situations or struggles make you feel most alone or unsupported right now?

\--

\--

2. Who in your life helps you feel seen, loved, and supported when things are tough? How can you lean on them more?

\--

\--

3. When have you experienced God's presence and strength in a hard moment? What did that feel like?

\--

\--

4. What usually keeps you from asking for help: fear, pride, embarrassment, or something else?

\--

\--

5. How can you be a source of support and encouragement to someone who might be silently struggling?

\--

\--

You don't have to face hard things alone, and you were never meant to. God is your constant refuge, your safe place when life feels too heavy. His strength holds you up when you feel like falling, and His presence surrounds you when you feel unseen. The beautiful thing is that He often shows His support through the people He places in your life, the friends who check on you, the family who loves you, and the mentors who listen and pray.

Don't isolate yourself when things get hard. Lean into God's love and let others support you, too. **You are seen. You are held. You are deeply supported by the God who never leaves your side.**

Faith in Action Challenge

This week, take time to share one honest prayer with God about something that feels heavy. Also, reach out to someone you trust and let them know how they can pray for or support you. Remember, God's strength often flows through the people He places in your life.

Week 35

I Am Enough

"And in Christ you have been brought to fullness. He is the head over every power and authority."
-Colossians 2:10

Have you ever felt like you need to be more to matter? Maybe you are constantly trying to prove your worth by studying harder, performing better, or striving to be the perfect version of yourself. Perhaps you compare yourself to others and always feel like you fall short. You tell yourself, *"If I could just be prettier, more intelligent, more confident, or more spiritual, then I'd finally be enough."*

Here is the life-changing truth: **in Christ, you already are.** You don't have to keep striving to earn your value or prove your worth. When you gave your life to Jesus, He filled you with His fullness, completely and permanently. You are whole, complete, and enough exactly as you are. Nothing you do, or fail to do, can change that truth.

Think about what Paul is saying here: *"in Christ, you lack nothing."* You don't need more success, more approval, or more "likes" to be complete. You don't need to look a certain way or achieve a specific goal to have worth. Jesus, who has authority over everything, lives inside you. That means your identity isn't based on how you perform, how you look, or how others see you. It's based on who God says you are. And when He looks at you, He sees someone already enough, already loved, already whole.

Today, let this truth settle deep into your heart: **I am enough because Christ makes me complete.** Take a moment to write down the areas where you often feel "not enough" in your appearance, your grades, your friendships, your abilities, or your faith. Next to each one, write: *In Christ, I am brought to fullness.* Read those words out loud and let them begin to replace the lies that have been holding you back.

Then, create a small daily reminder: a sticky note on your mirror, a journal page, or your phone background that says: **"I am complete in Christ. I am enough."** Say it out loud each morning until it becomes your truth: **"I am enough. I am brought to fullness in Christ. I don't have to prove my worth. I am complete in Him."**

Reflection

1. What does it mean to you to be enough just as you are? How would your life change if you truly believed that?

----

2. Where do you most struggle with feeling inadequate: appearance, school, friendships, or faith?

----

3. What are you trying to add to yourself to feel worthy: achievements, approval, perfectionism? How is that affecting you?

----

4. How would you treat yourself differently if you fully embraced your completeness in Christ?

----

5. How can you remind yourself daily that your worth doesn't depend on comparison but on Christ's unchanging love?

You don't have to keep striving, performing, or pretending. You don't need to fix yourself or become more of anything to be valuable. In Christ, you already have everything you need. You are complete, whole, and deeply loved. Your worth isn't determined by how well you measure up; it's defined by who God says you are.

So take a breath. Rest in the truth that you are already enough. You are a beloved daughter of God, filled with His fullness and chosen on purpose. You don't have to earn what has already been given to you. **You are complete. You are loved. You are enough, right now, just as you are.**

Faith in Action Challenge

This week, whenever you start to feel "not enough," pause and say a short prayer: *"Jesus, remind me that I am complete in You."* Then write down one area where you usually doubt yourself and replace that thought with a truth from Scripture about your worth in Christ. Speak it daily until your heart begins to believe it.

Week 36

I Am Fearless

"For the Spirit God gave us does not make us timid, but gives us power, love, and self-discipline."
2 Timothy 1:7

Have you ever held back from doing something because fear whispered that you couldn't? Maybe you stayed quiet when you wanted to speak up, hesitated to share your faith with a friend, or talked yourself out of pursuing a dream because you were afraid to fail. Fear has a sneaky way of convincing us to play small and stay safe, hiding the incredible potential God has placed inside us.

Here is the truth that will set you free: **the Spirit living inside you is not timid.** The same Spirit that raised Jesus from the dead lives in you and gives you power, love, and self-discipline. That means you already have supernatural courage available to you every single day. You are not fearless because you are naturally brave; you are fearless because God's Spirit empowers you to move through fear with faith.

Think about what this verse really means. Timidity doesn't come from God. That voice telling you to hold back, to doubt yourself, or to hide your light? That is not the Holy Spirit. God has filled you with power to do hard things, love to reach beyond your comfort zone, and self-discipline to keep going even when it's tough. When those three things work together, fear loses its grip. Courage isn't about never feeling afraid; it's about trusting that God's strength is greater than whatever you fear.

Today, step into this truth: **I am fearless because God's Spirit lives in me.** Think about one area where fear has held you back. Maybe it's starting something new, speaking truth in love, or using a gift you've kept hidden. Write it down, and next to it, write this: *God's Spirit gives me power for this.* Before facing that situation, pause and pray: *"God, thank You for giving me power, love, and self-discipline. Help me face this fear with faith in You."*

Then say this out loud: **"I am not timid. God has given me a spirit of power, love, and self-discipline. I am fearless."**

Reflection

1. What's one specific situation where fear has been holding you back from stepping into who God made you to be?

2. How would your life look different if you truly believed God's Spirit of power, love, and self-discipline was working in you?

3. When fear shows up, do you rely on your own strength or on the Holy Spirit's power? How can you shift your focus?

4. Can you think of a time when God gave you courage you didn't naturally have? What happened?

5. What's one bold step you can take this week that requires faith over fear?

Being fearless doesn't mean you never feel afraid. It means you refuse to let fear make your decisions for you. God hasn't given you a spirit that hides or holds back; He has given you one filled with power, love, and self-discipline. That is His Spirit at work inside you, shaping you into someone strong, confident, and brave.

The next time fear tries to whisper "you can't," remind yourself of this truth: you already have everything you need to face it. The Spirit of God within you is greater than the fear around you. **Step forward boldly, speak courageously, and live fearlessly because God's Spirit empowers you to be brave.**

Faith in Action Challenge

This week, identify one area where fear has been holding you back and take one small step of courage toward it. Before you act, pray and remind yourself of God's Spirit within you. As you move forward, repeat this truth: *"I am fearless because God is with me."*

Week 37

I Am Joyful

"You make known to me the path of life; you will fill me with joy in your presence, with eternal pleasures at your right hand."
Psalm 16:11

Have you ever felt like happiness keeps slipping through your fingers? Maybe you are chasing joy in achievements, friendships, likes on social media, or the next exciting moment. Still, no matter what you do, it never seems to last. One minute you are happy, and the next, something goes wrong, and that happiness fades away. It can be exhausting trying to hold onto something that constantly disappears.

Here is the truth that changes everything: **true joy is not found in things; it is found in God's presence.** The joy God gives is not temporary or shallow. It is not based on how your day is going or whether everything is perfect. It is a deep, steady, lasting joy that comes from knowing you are loved, chosen, and never alone. And the best part is that it is always available because God's presence goes with you wherever you go.

Think about the difference between happiness and joy. Happiness depends on what is happening around you, but joy depends on who you are with. When you spend time in God's presence, through prayer, worship, reading Scripture, or simply being still with Him, He fills you with a joy that cannot be shaken. Even when life feels hard, this joy becomes your strength and your anchor. It is not about pretending everything is fine; it is knowing that even when things are not fine, God is still good and still with you.

Today, embrace this truth: **I am joyful because God's presence fills me with lasting joy.** Take a moment to think about what you have been chasing for happiness lately. Are those things temporary or eternal? Choose one intentional way to spend time with

God this week: listen to worship music in the morning, read a Psalm before bed, or pray during a quiet walk outside.

Write this down: **"My joy comes from God's presence, not my circumstances. I will seek Him and be filled with joy."**

Say it out loud: **"I am joyful. God's presence fills me with a joy that circumstances cannot steal. His joy is my strength."**

Reflection

1. What is the difference between temporary happiness and the lasting joy that comes from God's presence?

2. When was the last time you felt genuine joy while spending time with God? What were you doing, and how did it feel?

3. What situations or disappointments have been stealing your joy lately? How can you shift your focus back to God?

4. How does experiencing God's joy change the way you handle stress, sadness, or tough days?

5. What is one practical way you can create space in your day to spend time with God and receive His joy?

Joy is not something you have to fake or force; it is something God freely gives when you draw close to Him. Happiness may come and go, but the joy that comes from being in God's presence is unshakable. It gives you strength when you are tired, peace when you are overwhelmed, and hope when you are hurting.

So do not chase joy in things that fade. Let God's presence be your constant source of pleasure. When you spend time with Him, His joy overflows into every part of your life; your friendships, your attitude, your peace, and becomes a light that others can see.

You are joyful because you belong to the One who never changes, and His joy will never run out.

Faith in Action Challenge

This week, spend ten quiet minutes in God's presence; no phone, no distractions, just you and Him. Reflect on one thing that brings you joy because of His goodness, and thank Him for it. Let that joy fill your heart and overflow into how you treat others today.

Week 38

I Am Abundant

"The thief comes only to steal and kill and destroy; I have come that they may have life, and have it to the full."
John 10:10

Have you ever felt like something is missing in your life? Maybe you scroll through social media and think everyone else seems happier, prettier, or more successful. Perhaps you have told yourself, *"If I just had that one thing: more friends, better grades, a clearer purpose, then I'd finally feel complete."* It's easy to fall into the trap of believing that abundance means having more stuff, more followers, or more attention.

Here is the truth that changes everything: **Jesus didn't come to get you into heaven someday; He came to give you a full, abundant life right now.** That kind of life isn't about how much you own or how perfect your circumstances are. It's about being so filled with love, peace, purpose, and joy that it overflows into every part of your life. Abundance in Jesus means your heart is full even when life isn't perfect, because you already have what truly matters, Him.

Think about what Jesus is saying in this verse. There is a thief, the enemy, who wants to steal your joy, kill your hope, and destroy your peace. He will try to convince you that you are not enough and that your life is lacking. But Jesus came to do the exact opposite: to fill your life with meaning, hope, and joy that never run out. When you walk closely with Him, you begin to realize that you already have everything you need to live a rich and fulfilling life. His presence brings abundance that circumstances cannot take away.

Today, take a deep breath and remind yourself: **I am abundant because Jesus gives me life to the fullest.** Shift your focus from what you think you are missing to what you already have in Christ.

Make a list of blessings in your life: friends who care, moments of peace, opportunities to grow, and the hope you have in Jesus. You may be surprised to see how full your life already is.

Write this truth somewhere you will see it often: **"Jesus came to give me an abundant life. I have everything I need in Him."**

Then say it out loud: **"I am abundant. Jesus fills my life with love, joy, and purpose. I lack nothing."**

Reflection

1. What areas of your life make you feel like you're lacking or missing something? How does the enemy use those thoughts to steal your joy?

2. How would your daily outlook change if you genuinely believed you already have an abundant life in Christ?

3. What does "life to the full" look like for you emotionally, spiritually, or relationally?

4. In what ways have you experienced God's abundance that has nothing to do with money or material things?

5. How can you share your abundance with someone who might be feeling empty or left out?

Abundance isn't about collecting more; it's about recognizing the fullness you already have in Jesus. The world will always tell you to chase more: more likes, more clothes, more accomplishments. But Jesus invites you to rest in enough. His love, His peace, His purpose, and His presence are more than enough to fill your heart.

You don't have to live with a mindset of lack or comparison. Instead, live with gratitude, knowing that your life is already overflowing with God's goodness. Every day is an opportunity to experience His abundance, not because everything is perfect, but because He is perfect. **You are abundant because you belong to Jesus, and in Him, you already have more than enough.**

Faith in Action Challenge

This week, write down three ways you have seen God's abundance in your life, big or small, and thank Him for each one. Then look for one opportunity to share that abundance with someone else through kindness, generosity, or encouragement. Let gratitude open your eyes to how full your life already is.

Week 39

I Am Limitless

"'What do you mean, "If I can"?' Jesus asked. 'Everything is possible for one who believes.'"
Mark 9:23

Have you ever talked yourself out of something before you even tried? Maybe you've looked at a big dream and thought, *"There's no way I could do that."* Or perhaps you've compared yourself to someone else and decided you don't measure up. Sometimes we build invisible walls of fear and *'I can't'* in our minds, and before we realize it, those walls start to box us in.

Here is the truth that changes everything: **With God, you are limitless.** When Jesus said, "Everything is possible for one who believes," He wasn't exaggerating or trying to sound inspiring; He meant it. When you trust God and rely on His power, anything is possible. God's strength has no ceiling, no boundaries, and no limits. When you walk with Him, that same power works through you. The only real limits are the ones you believe about yourself.

Think about what Jesus is really saying here. He is pushing back on the word *"if."* When God is involved, *"if I can"* becomes *"when God will."* Impossible becomes possible. Your worth, your dreams, and your potential are not defined by your grades, your past, or what others think of you; they are determined by your faith in a limitless God. That dream that feels too big? God is bigger. That goal that feels out of reach? He's already making a way.

Today, step into this truth: **I am limitless because everything is possible with God.** Think about one limiting belief you've been holding on to, something you've told yourself you can't do.

Write it down, then cross it out boldly, like you are erasing it from your life. Next to it, write this declaration: *"With God, this is possible. I believe."* Then, choose one bold step you can take this week toward a goal or dream you've been too afraid to chase. It doesn't have to be perfect or huge; it just has to be faith-filled.

Say this out loud and believe it: **"I am limitless. With God, everything is possible for me because I believe in His power."**

Reflection

1. What dream, goal, or calling have you been too afraid to pursue because it feels impossible?

----

2. How would your daily life look different if you truly believed that with God, everything is possible?

----

3. What past experiences have made you doubt what God can do through you?

----

4. Who in the Bible inspires you with their faith in God's limitless power? What can you learn from their story?

----

5. What is one "impossible" thing you feel God is inviting you to trust Him with right now?

You are not defined by your limits; you are defined by the limitless power of the God who lives in you. When you stop shrinking your dreams to fit your comfort zone and start expanding your faith to match God's power, everything changes. He's not asking you to be perfect or fearless; He's asking you to believe. Because when you believe, mountains move, doors open, and impossible things become reality.

So dream big. Pray bold prayers. Step forward with courage. The God who created galaxies with a word is the same God working in and through you. **You are limitless because He is limitless, and His power is alive in you.**

Faith in Action Challenge

This week, identify one area where you've been limiting yourself and surrender it to God in prayer. Take one bold, faith-filled step toward that goal, even if it scares you. As you move forward, remind yourself daily: *"With God, nothing is impossible."*

Week 40

I Am Aligned

"In all your ways submit to him, and he will make your paths straight."
Proverbs 3:6

Have you ever felt lost or unsure about which direction to take? Maybe you are facing a big decision about your future or wondering what God wants from you. Perhaps life just isn't going the way you planned, and you can't tell if you have somehow stepped off course. When you are out of alignment with God's will, everything can start to feel complicated, chaotic, and uncertain.

Here is the truth that brings peace and direction: **When your life is aligned with God's will, He clears your path.** That doesn't mean everything suddenly becomes easy or perfect. It means you gain a sense of purpose, clarity, and peace, even in the middle of challenges, because you are walking in the direction God designed for you. When you align your heart with His, chaos begins to settle into order, and confusion gives way to confidence.

Think about what it really means to "submit to Him in all your ways." It's not just about asking God for help with big, life-changing decisions. It's about inviting Him into the everyday moments: your friendships, your choices, your habits, and your thoughts. When you stop trying to control every outcome and instead say, *"God, lead me,"* something shifts. God takes the tangled parts of your path and begins to straighten them. Alignment doesn't make life perfect, but it helps you move forward confidently, knowing you're where God wants you to be.

Today, choose alignment over control. Say to yourself, **I am aligned with God's will, and He makes my path straight.** Think of one area of your life where you've been trying to handle things on your own: a relationship, a decision, a goal, or a worry. Write it down, then pray: *"God, I submit this to You. Align my heart with Yours and make my path straight."* This week, make it a habit to pause before making decisions and ask, *"God, what do You want me to do here?"* Even in the small things, seek His direction first.

Say this out loud and let it take root in your heart: **"I am aligned with God's will. In all my ways, I submit to Him, and He makes my path straight."**

Reflection

1. What areas of your life have you been trying to control without inviting God in? How has that worked out so far?

----

2. What does it look like for you to "submit to God in all your ways" in your daily life?

----

3. Can you remember a time when you followed God's lead and felt peace or clarity because of it?

----

4. What fears or doubts make it hard for you to fully surrender your plans to God?

----

5. How can you create space in your week to pause, pray, and seek God's guidance before making choices?

Being aligned with God doesn't mean you lose your freedom; it means you find your proper direction. When you stop fighting for control and start trusting His lead, peace begins to replace pressure. You don't have to figure everything out on your own or stress about every step. God's plans are always better, and His timing is always right.

God isn't trying to restrict you. He's guiding you toward the best version of your life, the one He designed specifically for you. So invite Him into your decisions, trust His wisdom, and let Him make your path straight. **You are aligned with a God who sees the whole picture. Walk confidently knowing He is leading you exactly where you need to be.**

Faith in Action Challenge

This week, choose one daily routine like your morning scroll, a study break, or bedtime, and replace it with a short prayer: *"God, align my heart with Yours."* Ask Him to lead your choices and thoughts. Notice how peace grows when you slow down long enough to seek His direction first.

Week 41

I Am Calm

"He says, 'Be still, and know that I am God; I will be exalted among the nations, I will be exalted in the earth."
Psalm 46:10

Have you ever felt like your mind won't stop racing? Maybe you lie awake at night replaying awkward conversations, scrolling through social media until your eyes hurt, or stressing about grades, friendships, or the future. Your thoughts spin faster and faster, your chest tightens, and peace feels entirely out of reach. You want to calm down, but you don't know how.

Here is the truth that brings your soul back to centre: **God invites you to be still. Not just physically, but mentally and emotionally as well.** In that stillness, you meet Him. And that encounter changes everything. When you remember that He is God, sovereign, powerful, and entirely in control, your anxiety starts to lose its grip. The same God who rules the nations and sustains the world is holding your life in His hands. His presence brings a calm that no amount of worrying or overthinking ever could.

Think about what God is really saying: *"Be still and know that I am God."* He's not asking you to figure it all out or manage every problem. He's simply asking you to pause, breathe, and remember who He is. You don't have to carry the weight of your world or solve every situation. When you quiet your heart before Him, the chaos may not disappear, but it stops controlling you. You find peace because you're anchored in His unshakable presence.

Today, lean into this truth: **In stillness, I find the calm my soul needs.** Set aside five quiet minutes. Turn off your phone, close your door, and sit with God. Breathe deeply and let His presence settle your thoughts. When your mind starts to wander, whisper this truth: *"Be still and know that He is God."* Afterward, write down how that time of stillness made you feel physically, emotionally, and spiritually.

Say this out loud: **"God is in control, and I can be still. His presence calms my racing mind and quiets my anxious heart."**

Reflection

1. What usually triggers your anxiety or makes your thoughts start spinning?

----

2. How do you typically cope when you feel overwhelmed? Do you distract yourself, overthink, or talk to someone?

----

3. When was the last time you felt true peace in God's presence? What helped you reach that moment?

----

4. What makes it hard for you to "be still" in today's world? How could you make stillness part of your daily rhythm?

----

5. How might your stress level change if you genuinely believed that God is in control and you don't have to manage everything yourself?

You don't have to live with a constantly racing mind or a heart full of worry. God offers you something better, a peace that doesn't depend on your circumstances but on His presence. Stillness isn't about running away from your problems; it's about remembering who holds the power to handle them. When you take time to slow down and sit quietly with God, your thoughts begin to steady, and your heart starts to rest.

In a world that never stops moving, dare to pause. Let His presence quiet the noise, still your spirit, and remind you that you are safe in His hands. **You are calm because you belong to the One who brings peace to every storm.**

Faith in Action Challenge

This week, practice stillness once a day, even for just five minutes. Turn off distractions, take slow breaths, and sit quietly with God. Each time, thank Him for being in control and let His peace fill the spaces where worry once lived.

Week 42

I Am Open

"Ask, and it will be given to you; seek, and you will find; knock, and the door will be opened to you."
Matthew 7:7

Have you ever found yourself closing off from new possibilities because of fear? Maybe you've stopped asking God for what you need because you're afraid of being disappointed. Or perhaps you've turned down opportunities that stretched you beyond your comfort zone, or pushed your dreams aside because they felt too far out of reach. Staying safe feels easier than risking rejection or failure, but it also keeps you from growing.

Here is the truth that invites your heart to open again: **God is calling you to live open, to ask, to seek, and to knock.** He wants you to bring your hopes, dreams, and needs to Him with confidence. When you live with an open heart, you position yourself to receive the blessings, direction, and opportunities He has already prepared for you. But when you close yourself off in fear, doubt, or control, you risk missing the abundant life He longs to give.

Look closely at Jesus' words: *Ask, Seek, Knock.* Each of these requires faith and action. They are not passive; they are bold. God will not force His way into closed spaces or drag you through doors you refuse to approach. He waits for your openness, your willingness to trust Him enough to take the first step. When you ask, He listens. When you seek, He reveals. When you knock, He opens. Living open means believing that what's on the other side of saying yes to God is always better than what fear tries to keep you from.

Today, choose this posture: **I am open to God's guidance, blessings, and opportunities.** Think about one area of your life where you've been closed off, maybe in your friendships, future plans, or faith. Write it down. Then, write one small way you can open your heart this week, such as praying a bold prayer, reaching out to someone new, or taking a step toward a dream that feels scary.

Declare this truth with confidence: **"I am open to God's guidance and blessings. I will ask, seek, and knock, trusting that He will open the right doors in His perfect timing."**

Reflection

1. What areas of your life have you closed off to God or to others? Why do you think those walls are there?

----

2. What is one thing you need from God right now that you've been too afraid to ask for?

----

3. Is there a new opportunity or challenge you've been avoiding? What has been holding you back?

----

4. How has staying in your comfort zone limited your growth or kept you from experiencing more of God's goodness?

----

5. What would it look like this week to approach your life with open hands and an open heart?

Living open doesn't mean living without boundaries; it means living without fear. It means being brave enough to ask God for what you need, humble enough to seek His wisdom, and bold enough to knock on doors even when you don't know what's on the other side. When you open your heart to God, you make space for Him to surprise you with His goodness and exceed your expectations.

Don't let fear or past disappointment close you off from what He wants to do next. God's plans for you are abundant, intentional, and good. **Be open. Be expectant. And watch how God responds when you ask, seek, and knock.**

Faith in Action Challenge

This week, ask God to show you one area of your life that needs more openness. Pray for the courage to take one step of faith, whether it's reaching out, trying something new, or asking boldly in prayer. Stay expectant and watch how He begins to open doors in ways you never imagined.

Week 43

I Am Safe

"I will say of the Lord, 'He is my refuge and my fortress, my God, in whom I trust."
-Psalm 91:2

Have you ever felt like the world isn't a safe place? Maybe you worry about the things you see on the news, feel anxious about situations at school, uneasy in certain relationships, or stressed about a future that feels unpredictable. It's easy to feel unsafe when everything around you seems uncertain or out of control.

Here is the truth that can calm your heart: **No matter how chaotic or uncertain life feels, God is your refuge and your fortress, like a shelter that never falls.** He's not watching from a distance. He's your safe place, your steady protector, and your constant source of peace. A refuge is where you go for shelter. A fortress is where you stand firm, surrounded and secure. That's who God is for you. His care doesn't shift with circumstances, and His protection cannot be broken.

Think about that for a moment. God is actively watching over you. He isn't ignoring your fears or minimizing your struggles. He's covering you with His presence, strengthening you when you feel weak, and surrounding you with His love when the world feels unstable. Trusting Him doesn't mean you'll never face challenges, but it does mean you'll never face them alone. His love is the safest place you'll ever be, and nothing can separate you from it.

Today, hold on to this truth: **I am safe in God's care, no matter what storms I face.** Think of one situation that's been making you feel uneasy, something happening at school, in your family, with friends, or even in the world. Write out Psalm 91:2 in your own words as a personal declaration: *"God, You are my refuge and my fortress. I trust You to keep me safe in [specific situation]."* Keep this note somewhere you'll see it, your mirror, journal, or phone, and read it whenever fear begins to rise.

Speak this over yourself with confidence: **"God is my refuge and my fortress. I am safe in His protection. I will trust Him and not be afraid."**

Reflection

1. What situations or circumstances make you feel most unsafe or anxious right now?

----

2. When you feel afraid, where do you usually turn for comfort or control? Does it truly help?

----

3. Can you remember a time when God gave you peace or protection in a situation that scared you?

----

4. What is the difference between trusting God's protection and expecting life to be problem-free?

----

5. What is one way you can practice running to God first when fear or anxiety begins to rise?

You are not at the mercy of a chaotic world. The same God who spoke creation into existence surrounds you with His presence today. When fear tries to convince you that you're alone, remember that you are covered, seen, and protected by a love that never lets go. Safety isn't found in having control over everything; it's found in trusting the One who does.

Even when the world feels unpredictable, you can rest in this promise: **you are safe because you belong to Him.**

Faith in Action Challenge

This week, identify one situation that makes you feel unsafe or uneasy. Each time the worry rises, pause and whisper, *"God, You are my refuge and fortress."* Write down every moment you notice His peace replacing your fear; it's proof of His protection at work in your life.

Week 44

I Am Free

"So if the Son sets you free, you will be free indeed."
John 8:36

Have you ever felt trapped by your past or your mistakes? Maybe you're weighed down by guilt from something you did, stuck in habits or thought patterns that seem impossible to break, or paralyzed by fear that keeps you from fully living the life you want. Maybe you care too much about what others think and feel chained by their opinions. You want to move forward, but something keeps pulling you back.

Here is the truth that changes everything: **When Jesus sets you free, you are truly free.** Not partially. Not temporarily. Completely. Freedom in Christ means that guilt, shame, fear, and regret no longer have power over you. The things that once defined you no longer do. You have been released to live the whole, joy-filled, purposeful life God created you for. You're no longer bound by your past; you're defined by His love.

Think about what real freedom looks like. It's not just *freedom from* something, it's *freedom to* something. You're free to live boldly, to walk confidently in your purpose, to love without fear, and to be your authentic self in Christ. Jesus didn't just open the door to your prison cell; He broke the chains completely. The enemy wants you to believe you're still stuck, that you haven't really changed, or that your past still defines you. But Jesus says otherwise: *"If the Son has set you free, you are free indeed."* That's not a hope or a maybe, it's a promise.

Today, claim this truth with confidence: **I am free because Jesus has set me free.** Think about one area where you've been feeling stuck, maybe guilt over something you've done, fear of what others think, or a habit you can't seem to shake. Write it down, then next to it write: **"Jesus has set me free from this. It no longer controls or defines me."** Whenever that lie tries to creep back in, speak this truth out loud and stand in your freedom.

Declare it boldly: **"The Son has set me free, and I am free indeed. I will walk confidently in the freedom Jesus purchased for me."**

Reflection

1. What specific fears, habits, or mindsets do you need to be set free from right now?

----

2. Why do you think it's so easy to keep going back to the things that once held you captive?

----

3. What would your life look like if you truly lived as someone completely free in Christ?

----

4. How does knowing that freedom comes through Jesus, not your own effort, change the way you approach your struggles?

----

5. What is one small, brave way you can walk in your freedom this week, something you've been too afraid or ashamed to do before?

You weren't created to live chained to fear, guilt, or shame. Jesus didn't come to make you slightly better; He came to make you free. The guilt you've carried is gone. The voice that whispers you're not enough is silenced. The fear that keeps holding you back has no power over you. You are a new creation, fully forgiven and deeply loved.

Freedom isn't about being perfect; it's about living like you believe you've been set free.

So stop agreeing with the lies that tell you you're still stuck. Lift your head, take a deep breath, and step boldly into the freedom Jesus already gave you. **You are free indeed. Live like it.**

Faith in Action Challenge

This week, take one brave step that reflects your freedom in Christ, whether it's forgiving yourself, speaking truth instead of fear, or letting go of something that's been holding you back. Each time doubt tries to return, say out loud, *"Jesus has set me free."* Walk in that freedom with confidence and joy.

Week 45

I Am Radiant

"Those who look to him are radiant; their faces are never covered with shame."
Psalm 34:5

Have you ever felt like you're just not enough, not pretty enough, confident enough, or worthy enough? Maybe you catch yourself comparing your reflection to filtered photos online or feeling self-conscious about something you wish you could change. Perhaps you carry guilt or shame from your past and hide behind a smile. You start to wonder whether anyone truly sees your beauty or worth.

Here is the truth that changes everything: **Your radiance doesn't come from what's on the outside, it comes from who you look to on the inside.** Real beauty isn't created by makeup, clothes, or likes on social media. It shines from a heart that's been lit by God's love. When you turn your eyes toward Him, His light fills you, and you begin to reflect His glow. The kind of radiance God gives can't be dimmed, edited, or taken away; it's the quiet confidence of knowing you are fully loved and wholly His.

Think about what this verse promises: when you look to God, when you seek Him, trust Him, and let His truth define you, shame loses its power. The insecurities that once made you hide can't hold you anymore. Instead, God's light begins to shine through you. It's not about perfection; it's about presence, His presence in you. True radiance isn't about being flawless; it's about being free.

Today, embrace this truth: **I am radiant because God's light shines through me.** Take a moment to stand in front of a mirror. Instead of picking yourself apart, look into your eyes and see someone deeply loved by God. Thank Him for one thing about yourself, something you usually overlook. Then say out loud: *"God's light shines through me. I am radiant, and my face is never covered with shame."* Write this truth on a sticky note or your mirror so you're reminded every morning who you truly are.

Declare this with confidence: **"I look to God, and His love makes me radiant. I will let His light shine through me, unashamed, unfiltered, and unafraid."**

Reflection

1. What insecurities or past mistakes have been dimming your light and making you want to hide?

----

2. How does comparing yourself to others, online or in real life, affect the way you see your own beauty and worth?

----

3. What would change in your confidence if you truly believed that God's love makes you radiant from the inside out?

----

4. Can you think of someone whose inner joy and kindness make them glow? What makes them radiant to you?

----

5. How can you let God's light shine through you this week in your words, actions, or attitude?

You don't need perfect skin, the right outfit, or a flawless high-light to be radiant. Your light comes from a heart that knows it is loved, forgiven, and secure in God's hands. When you look to Him instead of to mirrors, filters, or others' opinions, something inside you begins to glow. Shame fades, fear loses its grip, and joy takes its place.

You are radiant, not because you are perfect, but because you are His. Let that truth shine through you in every smile, every word, and every act of love. The world doesn't need more perfection; it needs more light. **And your light is exactly what God wants to shine.**

Faith in Action Challenge

This week, take time each morning to look in the mirror and thank God for one thing about yourself, inside or out, that reflects His light. Then share that same kind of encouragement with someone else who may need a reminder of their own God-given beauty.

Week 46

I Am Strong

"But those who hope in the Lord will renew their strength. They will soar on wings like eagles; they will run and not grow weary, they will walk and not be faint."
Isaiah 40:31

Have you ever felt completely exhausted physically, emotionally, or even spiritually? Maybe you're drained from juggling school, sports, and friendships. Or perhaps your heart feels heavy from family struggles, friendship drama, or anxious thoughts. You're trying to hold everything together, but deep down you feel like you're running on empty.

Here is the truth that breathes life back into your weary soul: **your strength doesn't have to come from you.** When you place your hope in the Lord, He renews your strength. That means He restores what's been depleted and fills you with fresh energy to keep going. Like an eagle soaring on powerful wind currents, you can rise above your circumstances, not because you're strong enough, but because He is.

Notice the rhythm in this verse: *soar, run, walk.* God's strength shows up in every season of your life. Some days you'll soar, full of confidence, joy, and energy. Other days, you'll run, determined, focused, and fuelled by faith. And some days, all you can do is walk, one slow, faithful step at a time. But through it all, His power sustains you. When you rely on yourself, burnout is inevitable. When you place your hope in God, His strength never runs out.

Today, rest in this promise: **God renews my strength. I am strong in Him.** Think about where you feel the most worn down. Maybe you're physically tired, emotionally drained, or spiritually empty. Instead of pushing harder, pause and invite God into that space. Pray honestly: *"Lord, I'm exhausted. Please renew my strength and fill me* *with Your peace."*

Then choose one small way to rest and recharge this week. Take a walk, listen to worship music, write in your journal, or spend quiet time in prayer.

Speak this truth over your day: **"Those who hope in the Lord will renew their strength. I will soar, run, and walk without fainting because God's power is alive in me."**

Reflection

1. Which areas of your life are draining you the most right now, physically, emotionally, or spiritually?

----

2. When you're running on empty, how do you usually respond: push harder, shut down, or ask for help?

----

3. Can you recall a time when God gave you strength you didn't think you had? What did that teach you about Him?

----

4. What is the biggest difference between trying to be strong on your own and drawing strength from God?

----

5. What is one small, practical step you can take this week to rest, refocus, and allow God to renew your strength?

You were never meant to carry the weight of life alone or prove how strong you can be. God offers you something better: strength that doesn't depend on your energy, mood, or circumstances. His strength lifts you when you feel heavy, restores you when you're worn out, and keeps you steady when you're weak.

You don't have to strive to be enough. He already is. So when you're tired, pause. When you feel weak, lean in. And when you feel like you can't go on, remember this promise: God will renew your strength. You will soar above what once overwhelmed you, run through challenges without giving up, and walk faithfully, one step at a time, with the God who never runs out of power. You are strong because He is strong in you.

Faith in Action Challenge

This week, identify one area where you feel completely drained. Instead of pushing harder, pause and invite God to renew your strength. Choose one action like resting, praying, or worshiping, and let Him refill what life has emptied.

Week 47

I Am Blessed

"Praise be to the God and Father of our Lord Jesus Christ, who has blessed us in the heavenly realms with every spiritual blessing in Christ."
-Ephesians 1:3

Have you ever scrolled through social media and found yourself wishing you had someone else's life? Maybe you've compared your clothes, your friendships, your body, or even your family situation and felt like you came up short. It's easy to get caught up in what you don't have and overlook all the ways God has already blessed you. Comparison has a sneaky way of stealing your joy and blinding you to God's goodness.

Here is the truth that can shift everything: **You are already abundantly, completely, and eternally blessed in Christ,** not with some blessings or a few blessings, but with every spiritual blessing. God hasn't held anything back from you. Even when life feels hard, uncertain, or unfair, you still have access to the richest blessings imaginable: peace, purpose, forgiveness, love, grace, and strength. These blessings don't depend on your mood, your success, or your circumstances; they are yours simply because you belong to Jesus.

Think about how the world defines being "blessed." It's often about having more: more money, more followers, more beauty, more recognition. But God defines blessing differently. His blessings are eternal, not temporary; spiritual, not surface-level. They are the kind of blessings that can't be taken away. Even in the middle of disappointment or struggle, you can rest in the truth that you are deeply loved, seen, and cared for by God. That is what it truly means to be blessed.

Today, open your heart to this truth: **I am richly blessed by God in ways that truly matter.** Take a few minutes to write a *Blessings Inventory*. List the spiritual blessings you often forget: God's forgiveness, His peace, His faithfulness, His constant presence. Then list the visible blessings in your life: your friends, family, church, talents, or opportunities. As you write, notice how gratitude begins to replace comparison.

Say this truth out loud: **"I am blessed with every spiritual blessing in Christ. God has not held anything back from me. I choose gratitude over comparison."**

Reflection

1. What spiritual blessings, such as peace, forgiveness, or hope, have you experienced recently that you might have taken for granted?

2. When you compare yourself to others, what blessings in your own life do you tend to overlook?

3. How does knowing you already have "every spiritual blessing" in Christ change the way you view your current circumstances?

4. What is one blessing, big or small, that you're most thankful for right now, and why?

5. Who in your life might need a reminder of how blessed they are? How can you help them see God's goodness this week?

You are not lacking, forgotten, or missing out. God has already blessed you with every spiritual blessing in Christ, not because you've earned it, but because you are His. These blessings are more profound than anything the world can offer and more lasting than anything you could lose.

When you start focusing on what you already have instead of what you think you're missing, your whole perspective changes. Gratitude grows. Peace settles in. Joy overflows. **You don't need more to be blessed; you already are.**

You are blessed beyond measure. Live as you believe it.

Faith in Action Challenge

This week, start a "Blessings Journal." Each day, write down three things you're thankful for, big or small. As your list grows, thank God for what He's already given you and look for ways to share one of your blessings with someone else.

Week 48

I Am Present

"Therefore, do not worry about tomorrow, for tomorrow will worry about itself.
Each day has enough trouble of its own."
(Matthew 6:34

Have you ever felt like your mind is everywhere except where you are? Maybe you're stressing about an upcoming exam, replaying awkward moments in your head, or worrying about what your future holds after graduation. Or perhaps you're so distracted by your phone or social media that you miss the people and moments happening right in front of you. It's easy to get so caught up in what's ahead or what's behind that you forget to truly live today.

Here is the truth that brings calm to your chaos: **God wants you to live fully in this moment.** When you're anxious about the future or weighed down by regrets from the past, you miss the beauty and purpose God has for you right now. Jesus isn't saying you shouldn't plan or care about what's ahead. He's simply reminding you that tomorrow isn't yours to control. God is already there. Your job is to show up today.

Think about it this way. Anxiety about the future whispers, *"What if everything goes wrong?"* Regret about the past says, *"If only I'd done things differently."* But God gently says, *"I've got tomorrow covered, and I've already forgiven yesterday. Be here with Me, right now."* Every day comes with its own challenges, yes, but also unique joys, blessings, and opportunities to grow. When you slow down and stay present, you start to notice God's presence all around you, in conversations, in laughter, and in small moments that might otherwise go unnoticed.

Today, choose this mindset: I will live fully present in this moment, trusting God with everything else. Think about what most often pulls you away from being present. Is it worry about the future, distraction, or comparison? For the next twenty-four hours, when your thoughts start to drift, take a deep breath and pray, *"God, help me be here now."* Let your heart rest in the peace that comes from knowing He is already working on your tomorrows.

Speak this truth out loud: **"I will not worry about tomorrow. God is in control of my future, and I trust Him. I will be fully present today, grateful for His blessings and confident in His plan."**

Reflection

1. When your mind starts to wander, does it usually go to past regrets or future worries? What triggers those thoughts?

----

2. What moments or blessings in your life right now might you be missing because you're not fully present?

----

3. What does "living in the moment" look like for you practically? What habits might need to change?

----

4. How does trusting God with tomorrow free you to enjoy today? Can you think of a time when you experienced that peace?

----

5. What is one thing happening in your life right now that deserves your full attention, gratitude, or joy?

Life isn't happening in your yesterdays or your tomorrows; it's happening right now. When you spend all your energy worrying about what might happen or wishing you could change what already did, you miss the gift of today. God's grace is enough for this moment. His mercies are new this morning. His presence is right here, ready to meet you in the now.

So take a deep breath. Put down your phone. Quiet your thoughts. Release yesterday, fully embrace today, and trust Him with tomorrow. **This moment is sacred because God is in it. Be present for it; your peace and purpose are waiting here.**

Faith in Action Challenge

This week, make a conscious effort to be fully present wherever you are. Put away distractions during conversations, meals, or quiet time with God. When your thoughts wander to tomorrow, whisper, *"God, help me be here now,"* and notice how His peace fills the present moment.

Week 49

I Am Unstoppable

"What, then, shall we say in response to these things? If God is for us, who can be against us?"
-Romans 8:31

Have you ever felt like the odds are completely stacked against you? Maybe you're staring at a challenge that feels too big, facing people who doubt you, or fighting through moments when giving up feels easier than pressing on. Sometimes life throws obstacles your way that make you wonder if you're really capable of succeeding.

Here is the truth that changes everything: **When God is for you, nothing can stop you.** You're not unstoppable because you have everything figured out; you're unstoppable because the Creator of the universe is fighting for you. When God is on your side, no amount of opposition can derail His plans for your life. Every obstacle becomes a setup for His power to shine through you. Every setback becomes a stepping stone toward His greater purpose.

Think about what Paul is asking here: *"If God is for us, who can be against us?"* The answer is no one who truly matters. That doesn't mean life will always be easy or that you won't face challenges. You will. But none of those things can defeat you when your faith is anchored in God. The One who spoke the universe into existence can move mountains, calm storms, and resurrect dead dreams. When you align your heart with His purpose, nothing can stand in your way.

Today, claim this powerful truth: **I am unstoppable because God is on my side.** Think about one obstacle that has been making you feel stuck; maybe fear, self-doubt, or something you've been avoiding. Write it down, and next to it, write Romans 8:31. Pray over it: *"God, I trust that You are for me. Help me take the next step with courage* *and faith, knowing You are fighting for me."* Then take one small step forward this week, no matter how big the challenge feels.

Speak this declaration with boldness: **"God is for me, so no obstacle is too great. I am unstoppable in His strength. I will not give up or back down, because the Creator of the universe is on my side."**

Reflection

1. What dream, goal, or challenge in your life feels too big to accomplish right now? What's holding you back?

----

2. Who or what has made you feel small, incapable, or discouraged? How does the truth that "God is for you" change that perspective?

----

3. Can you think of a time when God helped you overcome something you thought was impossible? What did you learn about His power and faithfulness?

----

4. What's the difference between trying to be unstoppable in your own strength and being unstoppable through God's strength?

----

5. What bold action can you take this week that reflects your faith in an unstoppable God?

You are not defined by your obstacles, your failures, or the opinions of others. You are defined by a God who fights for you, equips you, and calls you unstoppable. When God is for you, you don't have to fear what stands against you. That doesn't mean you'll never face struggles; it means you'll never face them alone.

So stop shrinking back. Stop doubting what God can do through you. The same power that raised Jesus from the dead lives in you. That power makes you brave, resilient, and unstoppable. Walk boldly into your purpose, chase your dreams with confidence, and face every challenge with faith. **Because when God is for you, nothing and no one can stand in your way.**

Faith in Action Challenge

This week, face one challenge you've been avoiding because of fear or doubt. Write Romans 8:31 somewhere you'll see it every day, and let it remind you that God is fighting for you. Take one step forward in faith, trusting that with Him, you are truly unstoppable.

Week 50

I Am Whole

"And in Christ you have been brought to fullness. He is the head over every power and authority."
Colossians 2:10

Have you ever felt like something important is missing from your life? Maybe you've tried to fill the emptiness with relationships, achievements, popularity, or the approval of others. You keep thinking, *"If I could have this one thing, then I'd finally feel complete."* But no matter what you chase, it never seems to fill that space inside for long.

Here is the truth that sets you free: **In Christ, you are already whole.** You are not missing anything. You are not broken beyond repair. You are not half a person waiting for someone or something to complete you. Through Jesus, you have been brought to fullness, completely whole, loved, and enough. The world will always try to convince you that you need more to be happy; more likes, more success, more validation. But the fullness you're looking for can only be found in Christ. Everything you truly need, you already have in Him.

Think about what this means. You don't need a relationship to make you feel complete; you're already complete in Christ. You don't need to earn approval to be valuable; you already have the love of the One who created you. You don't need to reach perfection to be enough; you already are, because His Spirit lives in you. Being "whole" doesn't mean you'll never struggle or need to grow; it means that at your core, your worth is unshakable. You're not waiting to become someone; you're already who God made you to be.

Today, rest in this truth: **I am whole in Christ; complete, full, and lacking nothing that truly matters.** Take a few quiet minutes to reflect. Write down the things you've been chasing to feel complete, maybe popularity, perfect grades, a relationship, or a particular image. Next to each one, write: *"I don't need this to be whole. I am already complete in Christ."* Then list what's true about you because of Him: loved, forgiven, secure, chosen, whole.

Speak this declaration over yourself: **"I am whole in Christ. I have been brought to fullness. I lack nothing that truly matters. I will stop searching for completeness in temporary things and rest in the permanent wholeness I have in Him."**

Reflection

1. What have you been chasing to make yourself feel "enough" or complete? How has that left you feeling?

----

2. Where in your life do you already feel whole because of your relationship with Christ?

----

3. How would your mindset and choices change if you genuinely believed you're already complete in Him?

----

4. When you start to feel "incomplete," what usually triggers that feeling? What truth from God's Word can you hold onto in those moments?

----

5. Who in your life is searching for wholeness in all the wrong places, and how can you gently point them toward Jesus' fullness?

You don't need to search for the missing piece to your life because, in Christ, nothing is missing. You're not a puzzle waiting to be completed or a project waiting to be fixed. You are already full because the One who makes you whole lives in you. Every spiritual blessing is already yours. Every promise of God belongs to you.

So stop striving to prove your worth. Stop looking to people or achievements to make you feel complete. You already are. Jesus has made you whole entirely, beautifully, and forever. **Walk in that truth with confidence. You are full. You are complete. You are whole in Him.**

Faith in Action Challenge

This week, whenever you catch yourself comparing or doubting your worth, pause and say, *"I am already whole in Christ."* Spend five minutes each day thanking God for the specific ways He has made you complete: your gifts, your faith, your identity, and His unchanging love that makes you whole.

Week 51

I Am Motivated

"Whatever you do, work at it with all your heart, as working for the Lord, not for human masters."
Colossians 3:23

Have you ever had days when you don't feel like doing anything? Maybe you're staring at a pile of homework, dreading a project that feels pointless, or dragging yourself through daily responsibilities that never seem to end. You want to care, but honestly, you don't. The motivation is gone, and you're stuck in that *"what's the point?"* mindset.

Here is the truth that can completely transform your motivation: **When you do everything for God, even the small stuff becomes meaningful.** Your schoolwork, your chores, your sports, your creative passions, everything takes on new purpose when you realize you're not doing them just for grades, teachers, parents, or coaches. You're doing them for the Lord. When your work becomes worship, your effort becomes an act of love toward the God who gave you your gifts and opportunities. That's where real motivation begins.

Think about what this looks like in real life. That homework assignment you've been putting off? Do it as a way to honor God with the mind He's given you. That chore you don't want to do? See it as serving God by serving your family. That project that feels boring? Give it your best effort as if Jesus Himself asked you to do it. When you shift your *"why"* from obligation to worship, even ordinary moments become opportunities to show excellence, gratitude, and purpose. You stop working for temporary approval and start working for eternal impact.

Today, remind yourself: **I am motivated by a higher purpose, and everything I do is ultimately for God.** Pick one task you've been avoiding, something small but necessary. Before you start, take a deep breath and pray: *"God, I want to do this for You. Help me work with* *excellence, focus, and joy as an act of worship."* Then do it wholeheartedly, not for recognition, but as a reflection of your love for Him.

Speak this truth over your day: **"Whatever I do, I will work at it with all my heart, as working for the Lord. My motivation comes from serving Him, not from seeking attention or rewards."**

Reflection

1. What tasks or responsibilities do you usually struggle to stay motivated for? Why do they feel meaningless or hard to do?

----

2. How would your attitude shift if you saw every assignment, practice, or responsibility as a chance to honor God?

----

3. When was a time you felt truly passionate and motivated about something? What made it feel purposeful?

----

4. What does it practically look like to "work for the Lord" in your everyday life at school, home, or work?

----

5. Who in your life models godly motivation, someone who gives their best no matter what? What can you learn from their example?

You don't have to wait to feel inspired before you act. Real motivation isn't about hype or emotion; it's about purpose. When you understand that everything you do can be an offering to God, even ordinary tasks become sacred. Your schoolwork matters because it sharpens your gifts. Your responsibilities matter because they build character and teach you to serve. Your daily effort matters because it's one way to say, *"God, I'm doing this for You."*

So stop doing the bare minimum to get by. Start working with passion and excellence, not to impress others, but to honor the One who made you. **True motivation isn't found in what you're doing; it's found in who you're doing it for.**

Faith in Action Challenge

This week, pick one everyday task: homework, chores, or practice, and turn it into worship. Before you begin, pray, *"God, help me do this with a joyful heart for You."* Notice how your attitude shifts when your focus moves from obligation to honouring Him.

Week 52

I Am Victorious

"But thanks be to God! He gives us the victory through our Lord Jesus Christ."
1 Corinthians 15:57

Have you ever felt completely defeated? Maybe you've been struggling with something you can't seem to overcome: a habit that keeps pulling you back, a fear that feels too heavy, or a situation that seems impossible to win. You want to be strong, but no matter how hard you try, you end up feeling like you've failed again.

Here's the powerful truth that changes everything: **Victory isn't something you earn; it's something God gives.** You're not fighting *for* victory; you're fighting *from* it. Through Jesus, the victory has already been won. On the cross, He defeated sin, shame, fear, and death itself. That means no matter what battle you face, you're not fighting alone, and the outcome is already settled. You are not a loser trying to earn God's approval; you are a conqueror walking in Christ's triumph.

Think about what this means in your everyday life. That anxiety that tries to control you? Christ has already overcome it. That temptation that keeps tripping you up? He's given you the strength to rise above it. That situation that feels too big to handle? His victory covers that too. Living victoriously doesn't mean you'll never face struggles again; it means you face them knowing you're already on the winning side. God's power gives you the ability to stand firm, persevere, and overcome. Every time you choose faith over fear, truth over lies, or hope over defeat, you're walking in the victory Jesus purchased for you.

Today, hold onto this truth: **I am victorious through Jesus Christ-no. No battle is too great for His power.** Think of one area where you've been feeling defeated. Write it down, and next to it, write:

"God gives me victory in this through Jesus Christ." Then ask Him to show you one small step of faith you can take this week to live from that place of victory.

Declare this boldly: **"I am victorious through Jesus Christ. His triumph on the cross is my triumph. No battle is too great and no challenge too hard, because He has already won. I will live as the victor I am."**

Reflection

1. What's one area where you've been feeling defeated or stuck lately? What's been holding you back?

----

2. How does knowing that victory comes from Christ, not from your own strength, change the way you view your struggles?

----

3. When has God given you victory over something that once felt impossible? How did that strengthen your faith?

----

4. What's the difference between striving for victory in your own effort and receiving it through Jesus' power?

----

5. Who in your life needs to be reminded that victory is possible through Christ? How can you encourage them with your story?

You are not defined by your defeats, your struggles, or your past losses. You are defined by the victory Jesus already won for you. You don't have to keep fighting battles as if you're trying to earn the win; you're already victorious because of what He's done. His victory covers your fear, your failures, your temptations, and every hard thing you'll ever face.

So stop seeing yourself as someone barely holding on and start seeing yourself as someone who has already been overcome through Christ. Walk boldly in that truth. Celebrate the small victories, because each one is proof of God's power working in your life. You are not fighting to win; you are living from a win that's already been secured. **Hold your head high, daughter of God. You are strong. You are redeemed. You are victorious.**

Faith in Action Challenge

This week, when you face something that feels overwhelming, pause and say, *"This battle belongs to God, and victory is already mine through Jesus."* Write down one area where you've seen God's power bring you a win, and thank Him for it. Let gratitude remind you that the same God who gave you victory before will do it again.

Closing Reflection

You Are His: Fully Loved, Fully Known, Fully Enough.

Dear Reader,

You've reached the end of this 52-week journey. Take a moment to breathe it in. Week by week, you've invited God into your heart and learned to see yourself through His eyes. You've discovered that your worth isn't found in what others think but in who God says you are. He calls you chosen, loved, and His.

This devotional was never about perfection, but growth. Each week was a chance to draw closer to God, to trust Him more, and to rest in His truth. You've faced challenges, yet your faith has grown stronger. You've learned to trade fear for peace, lies for truth, and pressure for surrender. That's the beauty of transformation.

Keep walking with God. Talk to Him about everything. Look for Him in quiet moments and in everyday life. When you feel unsure, remember His plan is good. When you feel weak, His strength will carry you.

And never forget who you are. You are loved without limit. You are chosen for a purpose. You are brave, strong, and complete in Christ.

The same God who walked with you through these fifty-two weeks will keep walking with you always. So lift your head high, trust Him, and let His light shine through your life.

You are a daughter of the King, and your story is just beginning.

With love and encouragement,

Robin

 Appreciation

Thank you for spending time with this devotional. My prayer is that these pages remind you how deeply loved, seen, and valued you are by God.

As you move forward, I encourage you to:

• Keep your Bible and journal close. Let Scripture shape how you see yourself and the world around you.

• Stay connected to people who encourage your faith, such as friends, family, mentors, or a church community who remind you of God's truth.

• Revisit these devotions whenever you need to be reminded of who you are in Christ. Come back on hard, confusing days, or when you need to hear your Father's voice again.

You are walking into a world that desperately needs light, hope, and kindness. The amazing thing is that you carry all of that inside you because of Jesus. Let His love spill out through your words, your friendships, your choices, and the way you see yourself.

My prayer for you:

May you grow in wisdom and strength, rooted in God's unshakable love.

May you walk confidently as His cherished daughter.

May your life shine as a reminder that others, too, are seen, loved, and chosen by the King of kings.

Remember, this journey doesn't end here; it's just the beginning. Keep leaning into God's promises and let His truth define who you are.

You are His.

You are enough.

You are loved—today, tomorrow, and forever.

With gratitude,

Robin.

Other Books by Robin Kite

If you enjoyed this devotional, you might also love these titles:

Devotionals

A 30-Day Devotional for Women: Renewing Faith, Purpose, and Self-Discovery

A 30-Day Devotional for Women: From Fear and Anxiety to Faith and Lasting Peace 5-Minute Devotional for Teen Girls: A 52-Week Faith Journey to Build Confidence, Find Joy in Christ, and Discover Your God-Given Purpose

Faith-Based Coloring Books

Today, I Choose Joy!: An Inspirational Christian Coloring Book Featuring 50 Positive Affirmations and Motivational Bible Quotes for Women, Adults, and Teens

I AM Chosen, Loved, and Strong: A Bible Verse Coloring Book with 50 Beautiful Designs and Inspirational Scripture Quotes for Women, Adults, and Teens

Your Faith Is Stronger Than the Storm: An Inspirational Christian Coloring Book Featuring 50 Positive Affirmations and Motivational Bible Quotes for Women, Adults, and Teens

Coming Soon: 52-Week Devotional for Moms

Share Your Thoughts

Did this devotional encourage you or someone you love to grow closer to God?

Whether you're a teenager, parent, mentor, or youth leader, your feedback matters! When you leave a short review on Amazon, it helps other readers discover the same hope, confidence, and joy found in these pages.

Every review, big or small, truly makes a difference.

Thank you for helping spread God's love and encouragement to others!

Amazon.com/author/robinkite

About the Author

Robin Kite is a Christian writer, speaker, and former educator with a heart for helping women rediscover peace, clarity, and God-given purpose. What began as a quiet practice of journaling and prayer during her own faith journey blossomed into a ministry of encouragement that now reaches countless women through devotionals and Scripture-based coloring books.

Her works, including the Amazon bestsellers *A 30 Day Devotional for Women: Renew Your Faith, Purpose, and Self Discovery* and *A 30 Day Devotional for Women: From Fear and Anxiety to Faith and Lasting Peace*, invite readers to find comfort in chaos, hope in waiting seasons, and renewed strength when life feels overwhelming.

Together with her husband, Robin also leads a nonprofit ministry established in memory of their daughter, offering practical support and spiritual encouragement to children and families in need within their community.

Whether through writing or ministry, Robin's mission remains clear: to remind women that their healing is valuable, their purpose is God designed, and their story is still being beautifully written.

Journaling Pages

5-Minute Devotional for Teen Girls